Editorial

T0294310

Now there's a quick consumer culture it's very rare that people read long books anymore. It's usually just quick interactions [...] so I think poetry is one of the best mediums we have for communicating our ideas.
—Wilson Oryema, multi-disciplinary artist and writer

'Poetry establishment outraged': such a headline would have struck the reader as ironic a couple of decades ago, when there was no *perceived* poetry establishment. If we had thought in 'establishment' terms, we would have identified several such, at war with one another and themselves riven by internecine squabbles. The words 'poetry' and 'establishment' seemed to exist in different registers.

What a change is here! The current poet laureate is joined by the dowager children's poet laureate (Michael Rosen), the Makars, National Poets and other worthies, protectors of an abstraction which grows more sacred and more abstract by the year. The latest outrage is the decision by Ofqual (the Office of Qualifications and Examinations Regulation – who named that poor baby?) to make the study of poetry optional for GCSE English Literature students next year, and only for a year.

Before we connive in civilised outrage, we might ask what exactly 'the study of poetry' entails in the current GCSE syllabus. A 'themed anthology' entitled *Power and Conflict* may be the set text: up to a score of poems, one each by poets from Wordsworth, Emily Brontë, Browning, Tennyson, Owen, to the present, represented by Hughes, Armitage, Duffy – a brace of laureates – and others, the poems various in subject and manner but all possessing a narrative line and relating to studyable 'contexts'. At GCSE level this handful of poems provides a sufficient metonym for 'poetry' itself. On Facebook one quondam GCSE student remembered being asked to enumerate ten ways in which love is like an onion in Carol Ann Duffy's 'Valentine'. The approach has as much to do with arithmetic or olericulture as with poetry. 'I am trying to be truthful.'

Ofqual adduces the distortions caused by Covid-19 as the reason for its decision. Students need accelerated education, to make up for lost months. Speed requires a slimmed-down syllabus. In *PNR* 254 we reflected on the impact the illness has had on the rate of poetry production (which continues unabated). It had already established itself in the Muses' domain. As against the frenzied increase in verse output, students (directed by teachers) will have a choice: to avoid it altogether. Shakespeare remains safe: a play must still be studied. But only two of the three remaining topics need be pursued: the nineteenth-century novel; fiction or drama from the British Isles since 1914; and poetry. Poetry has an advantage for the sprinting student. It entails the least reading... There is no 'fiction' or 'drama' establishment or Ofqual would have heard from them long ago about the either/or – as though there was some generic or qualitative equivalence. Poetry has had a louder institutional claque all along.

But not as strong as science. Kate Clanchy commented in the *Guardian,* 'The content of double science – the popular three-in-one science GCSE – is presumably also, as Ofqual says of poetry, difficult to deliver online, but Ofqual isn't telling teachers they can pick between chemistry and biology next year providing they stick with the physics. It would cause outrage: we all know that all three sciences are important. So what do we know about poetry? Cutting just English and the speaking elements of modern foreign language sends a wider message about the importance of these subjects, a message about who can be bossed and what is dispensable.' This begs the question, what is GCSE poetry?

Simon Armitage is worried that making poetry optional 'might have a knock-on effect and just make it one of those add-ons that it's been at times in the past'. At issue is poetry's reputation. But what is the *educational* value of what is being taught – the exiguous syllabus, and its outcomes? He says, 'Poetry is language at play, and a lot of the time in a school or classroom environment, students are expected to use language in a very rational, logical and informational way. To be denied the opportunity to think of language as nuanced and playful is a pity.' But playfulness in language exists in other disciplines, and to count ten ways in which love is an onion is 'very rational, logical and informational'. If playfulness were one of the outcomes, one might leap to the defence, but outcomes are described in staid, solemn terms. I lectured a few years back to a group of GCSE students about the poems of Philip Larkin, suggesting that they could be read without reference to the poet's life. At the end of my talk the teacher, thanking me, reminded the students that they had been provided ten biographical facts about Larkin that they must mention in their answers to the examination questions. Such an 'informational' approach did little to free up Larkin's poems for the young readers. There was no measuring the 'sense of play'.

This 'option year' may prove an opportunity to re-assess how, and what, poetry is included in the future GCSE syllabus, how to make it more demanding and rewarding a subject when it becomes compulsory once more.

Poets are emphatic spokespersons for keeping poetry compulsory at GCSE regardless of the educational crisis produced by Covid-19. They insist on poetry's popularity and relevance. If their arguments are true, poetry may not need to be squeezed into the Covid-foreshortened classroom next year. The limiting syllabus and the outcome-orientated impoverishment of exam culture can damage natural enthusiasm and condition the response of young readers. Their exam answers must be comparable and markable. Ten facts about Philip Larkin's life, ten ticks in the margin. Ten rings of the love onion.

Maybe a year of *voluntary* rather than *compulsory* GCSE poetry will be good for the art, the artist, the teacher and the developing reader.

News and Notes

Pinter Prize 2020

The 2020 PEN Pinter Prize was awarded to Linton Kwesi Johnson, a popular and timely choice, described by Claire Armistead for the judges as 'poet, reggae icon, academic and campaigner, whose impact on the cultural landscape over the last half century has been colossal and multi-generational'. He was characterised as 'unwaveringly committed to political expression' in his work. Armistead's fellow judges were Dialogue Books Publisher Sharmaine Lovegrove and author Max Porter. The award will be presented at a digital ceremony co-hosted by the British Library on 12 October – the day on which Harold Pinter would have turned ninety. Johnson will name his own co-winner of the award for the International Writer of Courage 2020, selected from a shortlist of international cases supported by PEN.

Gösta Ågren (1936–2020)

Christine De Luca writes: Gösta Ågren (1936–2020), who died in June, was one of Finland's most important poetic voices. Being a Swedish-Finn from Ostrobothnia, his poems, essays and biographies were written in Swedish. With his philosophical turn of mind, his poems often reflected on the complexities of being human, and of facing death.

He published several collections, reaching ever bigger audiences through the 1970s with Don't be Afraid and Cloud Summers. His major work was the Jär (Here) trilogy, the first part being awarded the Finlandia Prize in 1989. In 2011 Ågren was awarded the Swedish Academy's Finland Prize for significant contributions to Finland's Swedish-speaking cultural life and nominated for the Nordic Council Literature Prize, and in 2013 he won acclaim from the Längmanska Kulturfonden Foundation in Sweden.

I met him in Spring 2002 when, at Moniack Mhor in the Scottish Highlands, we participated in the first of the annual poetry translation workshops organised jointly by Literature Across Frontiers and the Scottish Poetry Library. Like him, I greatly enjoyed the opportunity to work with the poets and translators from Iceland, Norway and Denmark, along with David McDuff from the UK. While Gösta embodied the serious and the contemplative – so evident in his poetry – he was also convivial and sometimes, unexpectedly, uproarious.

His poetry has been translated into Finnish, English, French, Spanish, Icelandic, Russian, Dutch and Hungarian. *A Valley in the Midst of Violence: Selected Poems* (En dal i våldet) with translations by David McDuff, was published by Bloodaxe Books in 1992. As he wrote in 'Kvar'/ 'Left', one of the poems I translated into Shetlandic in the workshop:

> Naethin is left
> but your wirds, your hoose
> an your love.

Michael McClure (1932–2020)

Brian Morton writes: Michael McClure did not want poetry to be aethereal. He wanted it muscular, mammalian, meaty. His plane of art was the tribal dancing ground, his ethic a kind of hunter-gatherer spirit that snarled at the pastoral. He turned being lionised into an active verb when in 1966, a decade after his celebrated emergence at the Six Gallery readings in San Francisco which marked the beginning of the Beat movement, he read (roared) his poetry in the big cat house at San Francisco zoo. He was routinely described as leonine, but it proved to be more literally true than usual: the lions seemed to recognise his spirit and roared back competitively.

He had other claims on notoriety. He ran with the Hell's Angels for a while, celebrating the 'meat-spirit' of the tribal male. His play *The Beard*, which included a sex act between Billy The Kid and Jean Harlow was censored, even in tolerant San Francisco; when it transferred to Los Angeles, the cast was arrested every night of its short run, bailed just in time to go through the whole process again. If the younger crowd knew him, it was probably because he turns up in the middle of Martin Scorsese's documentary about The Band's farewell concert, The Last Waltz. He didn't opt to read from *Hymns To St Geryon* (1959), *Ghost Tantras* (1964) or *Love Lion Book* (1966). Instead, dressed like an exiled count, he recited the opening of Chaucer's Prologue to the *Canterbury Tales*. Middle and Old English – or what was then called Anglo-Saxon – fascinated him. One of his more notorious writings, in *Meat Science Essays* was a deconstruction of 'Phi Upsilon Kappa', the once vigorous Anglo-Saxon verb for coition that had descended into a catch-all, classless, meaningless obscenity. His own language was scarcely chaste, but never pointlessly obscene.

McClure was born in Marysville, Kansas, but raised largely in Seattle by his grandfather, after his parents divorced. The Pacific North-West shaped his view of wilderness America, even after he returned to Kansas for high school. He studied at the University of Arizona, Tucson, where he met his first wife Joanna Kinnison. They moved to San Francisco, with the vague intention of studying art and maybe movie-making. McClure was fascinated by Jackson Pollock's gestural, almost terpsichorean approach to painting, as photographed by Hans Namuth, but he was also drawn to the Black Mountain aesthetic of Charles Olson, with its emphasis on 'energy' and composition by field, and he found that his own creativity was more readily expressed in text and declamation than on canvas or celluloid.

McClure's poetry was, in the words of his friend, avant-garde movie-maker Stan Brakhage, a series of 'cellular messages', often expressed as surreal autobiography, as in 'Dream: The Night Of December 23rd' where McClure and dedicatee Jane remember watching giant extinct birds from Madagascar walking across a field in 1940s Wichita, 'sweeping / side to side as a salmon does – or as a wolf does - / but with a Pleistocene, self-involved gentleness / beyond our ken.' In 'Peyote Poem' – an inevitable experiment, though psychotropics were not, one feels, overwhelmingly important to him – he wrote 'I hear / the music of myself and write it down'. He listened outwardly and inwardly, and when he said, in the same poem, 'I know // all that I need to know' it was body-knowledge that he meant rather than learning. McClure won unexpected endorsement from Francis Crick, the co-discoverer of DNA's double helix, who quoted him in *Of Molecules and Men*, an association that reinforced McClure's belief that poetry and science were not at Blakean odds, but were part of the same endeavour.

He had more predictable associations with the rock crowd, falling in with Ray Manzarek of The Doors and creating in lead singer and would-be poet Jim Morrison an almost cartoonish version of himself. McClure later, after Morrison's death, performed spoken-word recitals with the pianist, releasing *Love Lion* (1993) and *The Piano Poems* (2012). McClure also wrote the lyrics to 'Mercedes Benz', an a capella hit for Janis Joplin. And he was present, an already senior statesman, on Thanksgiving Day at Winterland in San Francisco, as The Band brought it all home. Also on stage that night was McClure's one-time mentor Robert Duncan and his Hell's Angels mentor Freewheelin' Frank, whose autobiography he had ghosted.

McClure continued writing to the end, publishing nearly fifty poetry collections, plays and other works, appearing in films (notably Peter Fonda's *The Hired Hand*) and serving as a wise and well-loved teacher at California College of the Arts (formerly Arts and Crafts) in Oakland. Of all the Beat generation, he wore his own mythology most lightly. Jack Kerouac has him as Pat McLear in *Big Sur* and *Desolation Angels*, a Rimbaud type whose totem bird is the hawk, and as Ike O'Shay in *The Dharma Bums*. But McClure was too much his own creation to be a character in American's poetry's longest running soap. His life was spent, in words he addressed to Kerouac, 'wanting the huge reality of touch and love'.

John Furnival (1933–2020)

Greg Thomas writes: John Furnival (1933–2010), who died on 31 May 2020 at the age of eighty-seven, was a text-artist and visual poet (though he preferred to call himself a 'drawer') who contributed significantly to the international concrete poetry movement of the 1950s–70s, as well as to visual and sculptural movements such as Kinetic Art and Mail Art.

A product of the RCA and the late-1950s heyday of British Pop Art, John's operation at the boundaries of text and image have much to do with the early collage works of Eduardo Paolozzi or Richard Hamilton. But Furnival's primary compositional mode became the free-hand text mural. From the early 1960s onwards he incorporated his interests in post-war consumer culture, cold war politics, literature, myth, and wordplay into a series of dazzling text-towers and columns, most famously the various instalments of his 'Tower of Babel' series, which he began in 1963.

These and other text-based works were primarily celebrated as contributions to the international movement of concrete poetry, and John's work was included in all the major concrete anthologies of the late 1960s. However, as Bernard Moxham noted in his recent obituary (*The Guardian*, 17 June 2020), John was never entirely comfortable with the label of 'concrete poet'. Indeed, he described his first work in the 'Babel' series, *The Fall of the Tower of Babel* (1963), as an 'anti-concrete' work, expressing his scepticism about the ideals of linguistic minimalism for which concrete poetry stood. Comprised of teeming rows of text, the design was executed spontaneously, growing initially from calligraphic repetitions of the phrase 'Peace for the World' printed in English and Russian (Furnival had worked as a Russian military translator for MI3 during 1956–57). The gesture is typical of Furnival's politically infused, often acerbic humour. Other works of this period, such as his 1965 sculpture *Devil Trap*, are significant contributions to the 1950s–60s renaissance of Kinetic Sculpture, while his press, Openings, co-founded in 1963 with Dom Sylvester Houédard, produced text-based artworks for distribution by post in the spirit of the burgeoning Mail Art movement.

In 1960, John began teaching at Gloucestershire College of Art, which then had campuses in Stroud and Cheltenham. He also picked up teaching work at Bath Academy of Art in Corsham, and from his West Country base made contact with nearby poets and artists including Dom Sylvester Houédard, Kenelm Cox, John Sharkey, Charles Verey, and Thomas A Clark. Their loosely collective activities made the West Country an unlikely centre for the concrete poetry movement. And though this scene was notable for its homosocial membership, John produced work throughout his life with his partner, the textile artist Astrid Furnival. He also communicated with artists and writers spread further afield, notably producing collaborative works with important late modernist poets such as Ronald Johnson and Ian Hamilton Finlay.

John remained hugely productive following the fading of the movements with which he was instinctively associated. In 2010, he co-founded the press Openings-Closings with his long-time friend and supporter Bernard Moxham to reprint as much as possible of his vast catalogue raisonné. During 2018–20, Moxham curated a series of ARC-funded retrospective exhibitions, collectively entitled Lost for Words, held at Stroud's Museum in the Park and Ruskin Mill, Venice's Emily Harvey Foundation, and Bath Spa University's School of Art.

Reports

Life and the Novel

GABRIEL JOSIPOVICI

In the *Times Literary Supplement* of 5 June 2020, Elizabeth Lowry writes perceptively on re-reading *A Passage to India* during lockdown. She quotes from the book:

> Most of life is so dull that there is nothing to be said about it, and the books and talk that would describe it as interesting are obliged to exaggerate, in the hope of justifying their own existence. There are periods in the most thrilling day during which nothing happens, and though we continue to exclaim 'I do enjoy myself', or 'I am horrified' we are insincere. As far as I feel anything, it is enjoyment, horror – it's no more than that really, and a perfectly adjusted mechanism would be silent.

This, Lowry suggests, is what the novel is 'about' – everyone tries to explain 'what happened' in the Marabar Caves, both characters within the book and subsequently, the critics. The answer, she suggests (and suggests Forster implies), is – nothing. The novel is like John Cage's *4.33* – four minutes and thirty three seconds of silence (she says 'like a John Cage piece', but it is clear this is what she is thinking of, not any of his other works).

She quotes the famous remark from *Aspects of the Novel*: 'Yes... oh dear yes, the novel tells a story – and I wish that it was not so, that it could be something different – melody, or perception of the truth, not this low atavistic form.' And she suggests that it was the full realisation of this that led Forster, though he lived for another forty-six years, dying at ninety-one, never to write another novel.

I think both Forster and Lowry touch on something crucial about both life and fiction, but that the conclusions they draw are wrong, unless you want to distinguish between 'the novel' and 'fiction', which I don't think either

of them do (Lowry describes *Aspects of the Novel* as 'his chatty study of the art of fiction'). They are wrong because it is not that life is so dull that there is nothing to be said, but that life is – just life. That is why the most interesting art of our time – such as Claude Simon's *The Grass*, with its epigraph from Pasternak: 'No-one sees the grass grow', Beckett's *Waiting for Godot* and *Endgame*, the later paintings of Bonnard or Harrison Birtwistle's *The Triumph of Time* and *Silbury Air* – seeks to catch within the web of fiction or drama or painting or music what 'cannot be said'. Not, where fiction is concerned, so as to turn fiction into music, or melody, as both Forster and Lowry tentatively suggest A *Passage to India* does, but in order to give us access to this most elusive thing – life. Allows us, in Claude Simon, to see the grass grow, in Bonnard, to get a sense of what a long life shared consists of. There is nothing mystical in this, and it is something we all instinctively understand, but it is extremely hard to find the artistic means to catch it. You have, I suspect, to want to express it very badly indeed to work your way beyond the traditional means of artistic expression and find out how *you* can do it (and every good artist will find his or her own way).

Forster and Lowry share with other English writers, such as Graham Greene, both a sense of what the novel cannot do (and what they would so much like it to do), and a premature shrugging of the shoulders at this impasse. If one reads Graham Greene's *A Burnt-Out Case* and then his notebooks for that novel, *In Search of a Character*, one is struck by the way a fascinating and powerful idea is ruined by the instinct of the old pro for a good plot to 'bring it to life'. If one compares it to another novel set in colonial-era Africa, Robbe-Grillet's *La Jalousie*, one sees how a turning away from the normal novel's way of going about its business, a refusal of the 'oh dear yes, the novel tells a story', makes not for silence but for a gripping narrative about jealousy and colonialism and, yes, life; while Greene's acceptance of it turns the fascinating concept of 'burn-out' into just another (very good) page-turner. At least Forster, in his last novel, stayed with his instinct and produced by far his best novel – though both before and after, in commenting on the book, he perhaps misunderstood his own creation.

Echoes from a Conference on Crisis

VAHNI CAPILDEO

They keep trying to come in, a guard reportedly said. The lady and the man will not listen. They turn up at the door. They want to come up the steps. A little boy in a sailor suit is with them. They insist that they should be able to come in. What a job it is, looking after the place at night. It is under restoration during the day. He is tired trying to stop them from coming in.

The phrase 'colonial uncanny' has been haunting me, and not just in its academic sense. Not far away, Mille Fleurs, the marble and wrought iron mansion built in 1904 for Dr and Mrs Prada, and now government property, palely overlooks Port of Spain's Queen's Park Savannah where masked people exercise at dawn or dusk. Mille Fleurs had been falling apart for years, in contrast with the health-seeking, sweating bodies across the road. Lately somewhat restored, and secured at night, it continues to host tensions of ownership, between territorial creole ghosts and post-independence guards. The proximity between decaying refinement and straining movement recalls our genetic and/or cultural legacy from slavery and indentured labour. Yet 'colonial uncanny' spoke itself in my mind only when the 'pandemic uncanny' was invoked during a Zoom conference I attended on 26 June 2020. Zombies also received a mention.

This was the British Association for Contemporary Literary Studies (BACLS) conference on crisis. Two hundred participants registered, with the majority remaining in attendance throughout. Preparation for the online BACLS 2021 conference is already underway. Since the plague has changed how we can know each other, and intensified pre-existing differences, I have witnessed the eagerness of some attendees at online events for normality's return, when they can reconvene, or invite new friends. This was not a theme of the BACLS conference.

While eagerness to meet up is a sign of living hopefully, hope can be perverted into destructive channels. The thoughtfulness of the BACLS participants about many senses of 'crisis' laid the groundwork for new thinking. Perhaps this means that – rather than hoping for the return of rushing about by aeroplane and private car for short trips, polluting, consuming, touristifying – organisers will set an example, and embrace the lightness of distance and nearly carbon-neutral approaches; enhancing accessibility, too...

Virus-related anxiety belongs in a longer-running story of disaster: our species' addiction to anti-environmental ways of life. Lethal habits enjoy a flipped value, as if they were signs of our specialness and flourishing. We could activate instead a sense of 'crisis' deeply and ordinarily enough to modify our turning points. For the history of the word 'crisis' indicates judgment as well as event, decision-making as well as loss of control. It names the moment in illness that may lead to bettering.

Moreover, 'crisis', beautifully, is related to 'discernment' (via the -cern- element). At the BACLS conference, it became possible to discern many more different modes of understanding, and living, the applications of this small, supercharged word, while rethinking what personal experience might constitute 'crisis'. This piece will highlight details that implanted themselves in me and are changing my mind; without prejudice to those presentations left unmentioned. The aim is to give a faithful example of how one individual might react to the saturation of a day dedicated to the discussion of crisis; not to report from a reconstructed, ideal perspective. Fuller information is available from BACLS[1].

My first reflections are on the nature of the day itself as a prolonged moment. Attending a conference via Zoom (during extended lockdown in someone else's home) compels attention into unaccustomed forms. While I failed to be there for the 'real time' component of several panels, considerable material was provided in advance, on the conference website. At the time of writing, these audio recordings, documents, and slides remain freely available. Anyone interested can catch up later and re-play sections. Learning via replay has the kindness which slowness brings. You can pause, cross-check, and become unsocially absorbed. Notably, though, it lessens the feeling of things coming to a point – the crisis-like quality of energetic, ephemeral talk.

Is it universally acknowledged that listeners lose part of what they try to learn – it passes too fast? Are recordings therefore better than live participation – an improvement, not an alternative or supplement? Such a judgment, biased towards garnering information rather than engaging in thought, loses the importance of shared process, lovable in its nervy imperfection. If online events become the norm, how much would you miss companionship in velocity; complicity in falling from attention into distraction?

As with classroom teaching, so with conferences: the in-between matters. Knowledge is produced, and becomes memorable, when we mill about together. People need and deserve to chat informally about what they hear officially. When we interact freely and responsively, as mostly unlisted others, the analyses and information offered by presenters take on new, sometimes rebellious meanings. BACLS was the best of all possible Zooms, but Zoom lacks happenstance, even with an open chat room, an active lunch break, and the comradely interweaving of strands across panels. Like other online platforms, it feels high-exposure and up for 'capture'.

A move to e-participation need not strictly oppose knowledge to information. More radically, it will alter our 'normality', as regards the respective roles of authority and community in producing knowledge. It will affect how we actualise, and value, our potential for spontaneity. Time out to play/fight can be a phase of concentration. Any 'new normal' that sets efficiency above embodiment has a faulty metric for efficiency. Yet the 'old normal' of jetting around, often to picturesque, disabled-inaccessible places, was no good. What then? A blend of the hyperlocal and the long-distance?

Let us return to our known day of crisis...

A welcome effect of the opening roundtable was a feeling of time restored, the adjustability of self, and the lengthening of time. Novelist Sheena Kalayil relaxed our grasping after the immediate, calling the contemporary 'just a fleeting moment, a blink in the eye of the longer moment which is life'. The necessity of looking death in the face echoed through Dr Caroline Edwards's words. Dr Zayneb Allak, speaking on Han Kang's *The Vegetarian*, showed our interiority and exteriority sprouting into each other. Her reader is a Hieronymus Bosch-like creature, consumed by a proliferating novel. Ben Doyle, publisher for Literary Studies at Bloomsbury Academic Publishing, struck me the most, with his evidence base and his empathetic insight into the behaviour, prospects, and interconnexions of authors, academics, editors, and booksellers in Tempo Coronavirus.

Panel 1, 'Contamination, Contagion, and Crisis' was extraordinary. Checking my memory for continuing echoes, I find Liam Harrison on the 'untellability' of an ill person within an ill system resonating with Joseph Anderton, who was brilliant on the opportunity to use the crisis of the pandemic to re-evaluate other crises, but especially on the pathologisation of homelessness, and how the homeless long have been deprived of human warmth, as others avoid touching or looking at them. Mark Bresnan on the 'current infodemic', and whether losing oneself in conspiracy theories is a way of avoiding dealing with our all-too-obvious social affliction, violent masculinity, chimed with Sarah Collier's close reading of the 'trauma hero myth'.

Still in Panel 1, 'Plague Logics and Covid-19's Worst Hot Takes', Jennifer Cooke's presentation, gave me a paradigm for thinking through the coronavirus pandemic. Cooke observed that while community afflictions are not the same as individual diseases, and have unequal effects, the 'way the disease is perceived' is a risk to everyone. She explored how we understand the body and illnesses through metaphoric constructions.

Cooke rightly questioned the popular reactions that 'Nature is healing' and 'we brought this upon ourselves'. Some aspect of this may be factually true in terms of our poor stewardship of the planet. However, such attitudes unhelpfully belong with the same active and sturdy structure of revenge that has persisted since ancient times: God is wrathful; healers may be poisoners and make good scapegoats. Cooke critiqued the metaphorisation of language, a feature of 'plague logic'. 'Plague logic', as a style of thinking, seems orderly but in effect and in fact is unhelpful, even injurious. In tracing the barbed drift of terms that have gained currency – 'immunity' developed as a legal concept: exceptions that prove the universal applicability of law – Cooke gestures to the danger of casting everything as war.

Cooke's 'plague logic' echoed for me with Siân Adiseshiah's talk on 'Ageing as Crisis in Contemporary British Theatre', in Panel 3. Adiseshiah's incisive, poetic work remixed itself in my memory and haunts me in a series of tolling phrases, something like this. Crisis: instant. Crisis: impending event. Old age as risk, not opportunity. Crisis: moment. Disease. Recovery or death. Crisis: turning point. Better. Worse. Crisis: event. Large detrimental change. Crisis: lack of proportionality between cause and consequence. A small thing happens, in a short period of time. A structural breach. Radical transformative possibilities of rupture.

From memory's ongoing sampling of her conference paper, I select and highlight Adiseshiah's phrase 'crisis ordinariness'. She pointed out that 'crisis' has begun to shift to a narrative of 'what is'. This meaning of 'crisis' unfolds in stories of how to navigate the overwhelming. Here time lengthens non-restoratively, into a seemingly endless day of precarious existence, as with Benjamin's catastrophic perpetuation of the status quo. Crisis no longer names a rupture or turning point. In considering the revision of routines of what 'livability' might be, Adiseshiah looked at the co-production of old age and climate crisis. Older people are required to sacrifice themselves, to little effect. For crisis management (more of the same) is not crisis response (followed by transformation).

I hope this taster summary is enough to encourage you to follow up on the BACLS conference, which extended to four other sessions and lunchtime 'lightning talks', before the Live Writers Q&A in which I had been invited to take part. It was hard for me to speak. Zooming in from Trinidad to the UK gathering of intelligent, generous and kind thinkers, I felt weary beyond all reckoning; an affiliative weariness with those whose 'tongueless whispering' (in Martin Carter's phrase) animates these smaller islands. This was less to do with what was not there, than with the desire for my fellows to orientate themselves towards awareness of that absence, till it became more voiced, more collective.

Let's return to that phrase, the 'pandemic uncanny'. This was the subject of Helen E. Mundler's lunchtime 'lightning talk' on Margaret Atwood's *MaddAddam* Trilogy. Throughout the insightful discussion of whether or not a 'home', however temporary, can be developed or inhabited, there was no gesture towards how this resembles the 'colonial uncanny' (or, dare I say it, the 'white supremacy uncanny') in which much of world has been living for generations. When Mundler aptly stated that 'The Covid-19 virus, like radiation, is invisible and intangible, but wreaks terrible and often long-term damage; it is a cause of anxiety and an inability to live comfortably in the world', my mind antiphonally, rebelliously sang back 'magical realism is realism'. The magic realist texture of my current everyday is not only to do with diversity of spiritualities, créolités and habitats; but overarchingly and foundationally with this uncanny.

Here is an example of the 'crisis ordinariness' of our unacknowledged, shared context. A friend and I were sitting in the cinema in Port of Spain (during the Before Coronavirus years). Almost everyone on screen, in the trailers for films that would be shown in that theatre, was white. Almost everyone in the audience was non-white. I am not talking about the box-office-friendly casting of protagonists. The normed milky sameness extended to characters in the background of peopled scenes, where you would have expected a mixed crowd in real life. 'Post-genocidal fantasy', we joked incorrectly, in between awareness of the genocides perpetrated in our Americas, and what looked like wish-fulfilment elimination, or at least segregation, in our world to come.

It is no surprise, therefore, that after Megen De Bruin-Molé (Panel 2) delivered a magnificent paper on 'Living with the Crisis: 'Mindful' Consumption and the Rehabilitation of the Zombie in Twenty-First-Century Popular Culture', I went to look up 'real' zombies. De Bruin-Molé was merciless and funny about the political symbolism of the 'zombie' in popular film and TV depictions. The late-mid twentieth century zombie arrives in hordes to threaten individuals and individuality. (Hmmm...) The zombie of the 1980s is an oddball, a monster not unlike our misunderstood selves. Nowadays, the mindful, neoliberal zombie may work against organised, bad zombies...without escaping from consumerism, of course. But zombies are local, and the tongueless whispering in the land told me I already knew more and needed to know yet more...

The friend who had been with me in the cinema referred me to Mike Mariani's article for The Atlantic (2015).[2] In this piece, Mariani restores the heritage of the 'horror-movie trope': Haitian slavery. Haiti is a country of great culture, not too far away from Trinidad. I wish I could visit. There is a continuous strand of incredulity in my awareness about how this nation has been forced to service generations of debt, first exacted by France then administered by America, as punishment for winning a black liberation war of independence not long after the French Revolution. Mariani sees the initial 'zombie archetype' as a mirror of the inhumanity of slavery. Speaking of the 1625-1800 period of Hispaniola/Haiti, Mariani asserts that while those trapped in subjugated bodies 'believed that dying would release them back to lan guinée, literally Guinea, or Africa in general, a kind of afterlife where they could be free', suicide was not a permissible pathway. The spiritual penalty for taking one's own life was to remain on the plantation as 'an undead slave', a zombie.

The trajectory Mariani proceeds to narrate goes a little way to healing our knowing, even if nothing can be made whole. I laid it alongside De Bruin-Molé's narration of the trajectory of fictional bodies, strongly desiring a similar juxtaposition to happen as a matter of course, in reality, at the next such public conversation. To summarise Mariani: what he terms 'the post-colonialism zombie' refers to the post-Haitian Revolution period (1804 onwards). This was different from the trapped undead suicide. A reanimated corpse, made to work without reward or carry out dubious tasks, the post-colonialism zombie embodied 'a more fractured representation of the anxieties of slavery'.

Excision is how Mariani figures the zombie myth's disconnexion, in popular culture, from the memory of millions of African dead. The bodies and minds that do not fit marketable hero tales are cut out. His choice of word is telling. Amputation would have indicated the loss of a limb, i.e. something that was part of a body. Excision suggests the extraction of an alien growth. This chimes with the BACLS papers looking at how the language and logic of contagion have been used, long before the 2020 pandemic, to justify social exclusion. Mariani's attentiveness to the metaphorisation of language also is of a register with the day of discussion of crisis with which this essay primarily is concerned. What Mariani shows is that with this excision, we have lost any 'clear metaphor'.

What remains? 'Entertainment' and 'escapism' – not even true apocalypse, in Mariani's sceptical reading of the fictions featuring 'zombies'. End-of-the-world fantasies engage us in a refusal to confront real fears. Mariani concludes, 'Hence a bitter irony between the Haitian zombie and its American counterpart. The monster once represented the real-life horrors of dehumanisation; now it's used as a way to fantasise about human beings whose every decision is exalted.' For the stripped-down, brown-and-green landscapes of the zombie apocalypse give excessive power to the few remaining characters, feeding individualist desires for 'us' to make a difference – so long as 'we' can be significant, and saviours.

I agree, and conclude slightly otherwise. Before going out again on this heat-risen, rain-wet evening in Port of Spain to walk among the ghostly and perspiring inhabitants of Queen's Park Savannah and its neighbouring mansions, I find myself thinking of British 'nature writing' and 'psychogeography'. Ah, these increasingly well-funded, modish and respectable outsider genres. Never dare apply a political lens to the writing of the 'good guys', who elegise and/or empty their landscapes, forever writing loss, loving through lament and at best a kind of pained tolerance of change. Are these home-grown genres of excision? What tongueless whispering is accumulating in, and off the shores of, my adoptive land? May there be a crisis of transformation.

Notes

1 www.bacls.org/conferences/bacls-virtual-conference-june-2020/schedule-draft/

2 www.theatlantic.com/entertainment/archive/2015/10/how-america-erased-the-tragic-history-of-the-zombie/412264/

Some trees and some further trees

JOHN CLEGG

It's impossible to judge definitively from Google Earth, but I think that the white blotches visible in satellite view at 51°59'02.1"N 2°23'43.9"W are tree stumps; in which case they are all that remains of the trees written about by Robert Frost, in his poem 'The Sound of Trees' (from *Mountain Interval*, 1916). They were a clump of elms called the Seven Sisters, in Lascelles Abercrombie's back garden, at 'The Gallows', Ryton, Dymock (near Ledbury). Catherine Abercrombie had a 'permanent tent' there, and cooked duck and green peas in a cauldron under an open fire. A great number of Georgian poets came to visit, some camping out, others in spare rooms, others occupying the property when the Abercrombies were away: Edward Thomas, Ivor Gurney, W.H. Davies, Rupert Brooke, John Drinkwater who camped out but had to come back indoors because in the middle of the night he was 'blown on by a horse'. Presumably all the trees were brought down by Dutch elm disease.

A hundred metres east of the Seven Sisters is the edge of Ryton Coppice, a tiny stretch of woodland (a kilometre north to south, 500m east to west at its widest point), which has tangential connections with two famous twentieth century poems. Frost began to draft 'The Road Not Taken' at The Gallows in late autumn 1914; Steve Nicholls, in *Flowers of the Field: Meadow, Moor and Woodland* (Head of Zeus, 2019) has pointed out that Rydon Coppice is a particularly yellow wood ('Two roads diverged in a yellow wood') because its edges and clearings have for a long time been famous for their wild daffodils. (Children used to bunk off school to pick them, for market gardeners to sell in London.) The speaker of 'The Road Not Taken' has for a long time been identified as the vacillating Edward Thomas, and this is certainly a path which Frost and Thomas would have walked together in spring. If this identification is correct, incidentally, it's easy to identify from Google Earth the point at which the road diverges.

Nicholls may be pushing it a bit: the 'yellow wood' is surely also a close relation of the 'yellow leaves' in Shakespeare's sonnet 73, and the colour brings in the same thematic parallels (too late to change now etc.) – although I've never personally walked through woodland in autumn where the leaves felt yellow, quite. The twelfth line of the poem certainly doesn't seem to fit with daffodils: both paths lay under 'leaves no step had trodden black'. (That said, the grassiness of the path in the second stanza doesn't suggest November to me.) But the possibility is open, I think, that Frost had the springtime wood in his mind's eye when he began, which turned autumnal as the poem's theme developed. There is a reasonable possibility that the wood Frost had in mind when he began writing his most famous poem was Ryton Coppice.

Ryton Coppice is also in the background of Thomas's most famous poem. Around 1910, Lascelles Abercrombie wrote the long poem 'Ryton Firs', which he enthusiastically performed on many occasions at both the Poetry Bookshop in London and The Gallows. (He went on to add a post-war prelude, describing how the firs were cut down to be used as pit props for the Welsh coal mines. His *Selected* and *Collected* poems both print the poem with this prelude and revisions.) The final section of the original 'Ryton Firs', 'The Dance', takes as a repeating burden the line 'In Herefordshire and Glostershire'; I think there's a very good chance that this suggested to Thomas the final line of 'Adlestrop'. Further, more speculatively: I think Thomas heard Abercrombie read the poem, hamming it up, and realised how well the line would work if it was more subdued. Abercrombie rhymed 'Glostershire' with 'fire'; Thomas, 'Gloucestershire' with 'mistier'.

Anyway, this all unnerves me slightly, because all three poems, 'Adlestrop' and 'The Sound of Trees' and 'The Road Not Taken', are much too close for comfort. 'The Road not Taken' and 'The Sound of Trees' are the first and last poems, respectively, in *Mountain Interval*, announcing and tying up the book's concerns.

> They are that that talks of going
>   But never gets away,

writes Frost about the trees, but Thomas might have equally written it about the train; both poems have humanized and vulnerable cloud-formations; both poems address the irresolvable demands between movement and stasis, and how each is enacted in language (the fixed 'name' in 'Adlestrop', the false 'talk' in 'The Sound of Trees'). When Thomas idled in Adlestrop, he was heading towards Ryton to meet Frost. When Frost 'set forth for somewhere' (via London), he would have passed through Adlestrop himself.

Letter From Wales

SAM ADAMS

As an organisation, *Yr Academi Gymreig*, or *'Academi'*, the banner under which the Welsh Academy of writers has operated since 1998, appears moribund. I hope this is a misapprehension occasioned by my failure to keep abreast of its activities, and that writers continue to meet socially and to participate together in literary events. The last such occasion in which I had a part to play was in June 2009: a bus tour with talks of places associated with Roland Mathias. Led by John Pikoulis, biographer of Alun Lewis and then Chair of the English-language section of *Academi*, it was one of a series that also included visits to what one might call Raymond Williams country, around Pandy near Abergavenny, and Alun Lewis's Aberdare. The buses started from Cardiff, picked up paying customers en route and were invariably well filled with people (mostly of mature years, it must be conceded) who were knowledgeable and interested. The Roland Mathias tour took us to the Plough Chapel in Brecon, to the grave of Henry Vaughan in the churchyard at Llansantffraed, and to Talybont-on-Usk, its reservoir lapping at the tumbled stones of the poet's birthplace. It will be a grievous loss if this kind of experience is no longer offered to a public hungry for poems.

I have written before about the Welsh Academy of writers, which had its origins in conversations between two giants of twentieth-century Welsh-language literature, Bobi Jones and Waldo Williams. Their intention was to gather support for a new magazine to serve the distinctive literary culture that they exemplified brilliantly and an organisation that would enrol and represent writers in the first language of Wales. The *Oxford Companion to the Literature of Wales* notes that the choice of the more generally applicable adjective *Cymreig* in the original title, rather than *Cymraeg,* which applies only to the Welsh language, was designed 'to allow the subsequent inclusion of writers in English'. That is, indeed, what happened, when in 1968 the English-language section was formed at the instigation of Meic Stephens, then Literature Director of the Welsh Arts Council.

In the early 1970s, I thought myself peculiarly favoured to be elected to membership of *Yr Academi Gymreig*, to attend and contribute to readings, lectures and conferences along with other writers, many of them already acquaintances by correspondence, thanks to my role as reviews editor of *Poetry Wales.* An unforeseen and happy consequence of having re-settled in Wales in 1966 within a short distance of Cardiff was to find that, among the writers Meic had in mind when he wrote, in *Poetry Wales* (Winter 1967), of a 'second flowering' of Anglo-Welsh writing, several lived in or near the capital, or within a short, if tortuous, drive up the Valleys. I remember especially Roland Mathias on the outer rim in Brecon, and Glyn Jones, John Ormond and John Tripp, all at the time Cardiffians; then Dannie Abse could be found enjoying a breath of fresh air at his Welsh HQ in Ogmore-by-Sea,

Leslie Norris turned up on poetic missions from Sussex, and Harri Webb rolled downhill from Cwmbach. I admired their work and enjoyed their company, which was always stimulating and occasionally, thanks to John Tripp, verbally explosive.

The centenary of Harri Webb's birth falls in September. He came from a Swansea working-class background, and a family with roots in farming on the Gower peninsula, to win a place at Magdalen College, Oxford, where he studied medieval and modern languages, specialising in French and Spanish. (And in 1947, 'in three months of hard work [he] learned Welsh'.) During the war he served in the navy in the Mediterranean theatre, where he acted as an interpreter with the Free French, and in the North Atlantic. On shore leave in Scotland he encountered the writings of Hugh MacDiarmid, which introduced and quickly committed him to republican nationalist politics. After demob in 1946, early work as a librarian and bookseller took him to genteel Malvern and Cheltenham, but he was already a polemicist for *The Welsh Republican*, a bi-monthly newspaper, and in 1953 became its (unpaid) editor until the collapse of both newspaper and movement in 1957. In 1954 he returned to Wales as a librarian, first in Dowlais, Merthyr and, a decade on, at Mountain Ash where he remained until retirement in 1974.

The Merthyr connection is important. Harri was already a resident at Garth Newydd, a large house in the town, abandoned and apparently ownerless, when in the summer of 1962, on a day out in Cardiff, he first met Meic Stephens enjoying a pint at a the Old Arcade, a venerable hostelry. They fell into conversation and soon found they had much in common, linguistically and politically. There and then the budding relationship underwent a baptism of fire. A relic of Cardiff's great Edwardian coal-exporting days, the bar where the two were leaning had a small gas lighter above counter height where wealthy customers would lean to the flame to light their cigars. Engrossed in discussion, Meic was unaware his jacket had come within range of this unusual facility until Harri poured a pint over the smouldering leather patch on his sleeve. Meic, in search of lodgings within easy reach of Ebbw Vale, where he was about to take up a teaching appointment at the local grammar school, was delighted to accept Harri's invitation to join communal life at Garth Newydd. *Poetry Wales* and a great deal more derive from that chance encounter at the 'Old A'. It was Harri Webb who suggested to *Yr Academi Gymreig* that it should sponsor the compilation and publication of what became the *Oxford Companion to the Literature of Wales.*

He was well known as a polemicist to readers of *The Welsh Republican* and, later, to those of Plaid Cymru's newspaper *Welsh Nation*, which he also edited. His poems began appearing in *Poetry Wales* in 1965, and in 1969 his first book, *The Green Desert*, won a Welsh Arts Council prize. It was followed by *A Crown for Branwen* (1974), *Ram-*

page and Revel (1977) and *Poems and Points* (1983). The last named was a collection of verses, clever, humorous and scurrilous, many marked by the same trenchant wit that characterised his polemical writing, which had featured in, or been inspired by the opportunity of writing for, the HTV television show 'Poems and Pints'. Some of his squibs incorporating clever use of the demotic have been absorbed into the culture, while his song 'Colli Iaith' ('Losing Language', with music by Meredydd Evans) has become a regular feature of the National Eisteddfod. His *Collected Poems*, edited by Meic Stephens, which appeared posthumously in 1995, revealed a prolific verse writer and an accomplished prosodist, notably in the sequence 'Sonnets for Mali', two of which not only fulfil the metrical requirements of the form but are also macaronic acrostics, the final letters of lines forming appeals in Welsh, '*Tyrd yn ôl gariad*' ('Come back, darling') and '*Dere lan eto Mali*' ('Come up again Mali'). He died in 1994. In characterising a fellow republican (the wife of a friend) whom he felt he strongly resembled, he offered a moment of self-analysis: 'subjective, romantic, loquacious, artistic, over-personal, with a talent for mimicry, a creative urge, and a too-ready tongue'. His wit was, indeed, sharp and could be merciless. It is said he had his faults (don't we all?), but in my experience he was a man of considerable charm and good humour. In the 1970s and 80s, he was unquestionably the best known and most popular living poet in Wales.

Here one begins again
From the Journals, 26 July 1999
R. F. LANGLEY

I will keep something of a journal, though much deters me. We are here looking for a house to buy. Pinfold Hill[1] is, subject to contract, sold.[2] I am retired. B has left her school-teaching job. We have until October[3] to find somewhere to live. Already we have spent a Saturday here, looking at five or six houses, with no luck, and a day in Shropshire looking at two more.

Here we are again in this two-bed guest room,[4] the sash window raised six inches, a grey squirrel jerking and flirting on the windowsill outside, house martins shooting across, cool, unshining trees, distant fields, Virginia creeper draping both sides of the glass; pale turquoise, seven o'clock sky with mushroom pink ceiling, B's words sounding with a factual crack and snap in the stillness, the wood pigeons silent after hours of intense calling - no, here one begins again, ending on the lame raised note. Then another, a higher pitched voice, not so much urgent, or soothing, as mindless.

I awoke with an image of a plastic, transparent jug with thick frothed liquid in it, and I was trying to clear the froth by scraping it up the sides of the vessel with a thin rod – laborious, useless, futilely misjudged task. Oh dear.

A hollowness. The country has gone foreign. The stillness is one of incredulity. I am cheating everyone by being here. I would much prefer to stay put in the Midlands. This is jeopardy, the good place drained. I can't separate duty from fear, estimate the real worth of distance, of friendship, of acquaintance, of familiarity or the authenticity of my thoughts, my feelings.

Close to, the slat blinds hoist, scraping, on their cords, four martins flutter and fall away from the gutter without touching the immediate, factual world which I pass in. A scrape. A chirp.

A lapse into stultification, tinged by anger, as I drive, talk, smile. On a bye-road in Dunwich Forest on our way to the beach, we take a late picnic instead of going to a pub. I can't hear the grasshoppers until I stoop near one. A green woodpecker derides.

B walks on the grass with a mobile phone, testing it, calling Sue, who isn't in, calling Peter, who is. Four hours' drive away.

What should I be doing about all this? I need a guardian angel, a daemon,[5] some other self to trust and consult. Other people's needs swarm just out of focus. As I think of one it steadies, swells, occupies the field. I return to the static between demands, and there is the background world, unresonant, buzzing with flies, one of which bites B under her ear, flapping with big pigeons, curbed by gulls, lapsing in a backward fall into letting it go, like the loose twigs of a willow, dropped by the swell of the wind, by the pond at Westleton as we sit at a table at the White Horse once more,[6] at evening the thirty or more swifts hung up high, sheering away below the massive, surging clouds, lemon against the light blue. Low sun comes under the wings and glints. Mr and Mrs Coke looked bland and non-committal this afternoon. I must make up my own mind. There is no such thing as a mind.

Edited by Barbara Langley, July 2020

Notes

1 Our house in Shenstone, Lichfield, Staffs, no 57 Pinfold Hill.
2 In the end, those buyers withdrew, leaving us to resell quickly... but...
3 ... the new buyers insisted that we complete the sale and move out a month earlier than we had said we could manage.
4 The Old Vicarage, Walpole, Suffolk.
5 RFL didn't owe this concept or term to Philip Pullman, whose first novel in the *His Dark Materials* trilogy was published five years later, in 1995.
6 The tomb sculpture of Arthur and Elizabeth Coke by Nicholas Stone ('extremely progressive for its date, 1629, Pevsner, 1974) in St Andrew's parish church, Bramfield, Suffolk, the subject of many of RFL's detailed journal entries since their start, and of his 1974 poem *The Ecstasy Inventories*, based on the inventories of their possessions when they died.

Poems and Features

Two Poems

NYLA MATUK

Clouds

Watching the guard at the Viennese design museum,
his unknowing gathering, rising. He asks us where we are from, *really.*
We might have asked the same, but didn't.
We may seem a system of particles, familiar
from afar. Yet we're strange when you take a closer look,
like his *trompe l'oeil* ingress. He paces as a hover of droplets drops
the whole spectrum of light and electric energy down on us.
Our thoughts hold, with headroom. Once lost to us, they let us get lost, too.
Everything in the gallery is finely developed but trepidatious.
The objective of the game is not to speak
each other into existence, in any part.
Not to advance as a universal symbol
or presage bad times ahead. These lucid corridors lead
to a false infinity – certainty. Even a history of fog.
They are historic, tragedies pre-arranged. Forgettable,
the fog of an afternoon long ago at a ballpark, the candy floss of Sunday,
of a bath and a Disney show. Beams of sunshine
direct consciousness toward the will to be perplexed.
Unknowing is the product of
what yields power over us, the capricious clap
of sudden activity. 'Where are you from?' is dread,
finally revealed, dislike that they don't recognize us,
that dislike being unpleasant. He's the opposite of shimmering,
floating between rooms. He sits uncomfortably
in this unknown storm, a cage offering no relief. He judges and fears
unknowable self and others, and thinks everyone unpredictable,

though this is what might help us all escape. The proper application
of irony is a bridge too far.
And take that Chicago novelist who wants to know where
we are from, because he thinks we are like him:
we are not like either one of them. Not like the security guard who hates us,
in all our mystery. Is our mystery, to the novelist, our wonder?
Our affinity with these jars from Cathay? And is he prepared to like us
if we answer his question and conform to his ideal – that is, himself?
We'll never know. We do not choose to be pinned like butterflies to boards.
Do they want to know where we're from in order to confirm
our strangeness, our distant rumble of a bottled atmosphere,
our state in nature, our enigma, a multivalent affect,
a jewelry box crammed with costume brooches of flowers,
poodles, and Easter baskets? In order to give themselves
the discount of a given quantity in a thundering, dangerous location?
They're doomed to wander from vestibule to atrium
wondering.

Privilege

Tonight, they're fashioning currency with filigree
of rococo swans in green and plum,
   Polynesian plumage, carnelian, and hibiscus.
Night and labour and limitless mimesis. Its license
senses weakness. It will be used to kill.
   What was once public is now private;
outside a hedged garden unseen under hidden lock and key,
   a dozen TVs flicker at the commons while
      winter continues like a mid-century miniseries.
Whatever the ghostly last episode, the production affects the lives of millions,
   but never us, always them in their impressive bravery, their children
sleeping by the squawk of the night radio, the bar crowd downstairs.
   As if everything was easily forgettable, coats are hung up for the night
without consequence, a bourgeoisie of calling in dead.
   An army and bureaucracy for others, not us. The bank tower's
blank mirrors stare at the tea-rose dusk, romance unending worth. A revered river of light.
   There is no mandate for a god who stands outside the trade in illusion.
Cars continue on that ring road outside town, an unceasing ocean,
   heard but not seen. Never seen.

Sides Unseen

The David Zwirner Books Ekphrasis Series

JENA SCHMITT

A friend first pointed out Rilke's *Letters to a Young Painter* at a bookshop in Toronto. Months later – after seeing a statue of St. Catherine of Alexandria stepping on the head of Emperor Maxentius – a table with birds' feet by Meret Oppenheim – Rachel Krobone's *399 Days*, with its orgiastic tangle of limbs that references Ovid, Dante, Michelangelo and Bernini – a clever floral bouquet made of glinting petal-like profusions of silverware (Ann Carrington, 2016) – and the vast expanse of the Ardabil Carpet – on a Friday evening at the V&A, I happened upon South Kensington Books, where, along with the Rilke, there was Marcel Proust's *Chardin and Rembrant*, Vernon Lee's *The Psychology of an Art Writer*, and John Ruskin's *Giotto and His Works in Padua*. (You must bear with me, I live in a small town where the only bookshop is in a strip mall with every second or third store boarded up and for lease. To occasionally find myself in a place where I might walk freely into a shop with an abundance of books or a space brimming with art still fills me with excitement.)

Rilke and Proust, Lee and Ruskin are part of the David Zwirner Books ekphrasis series, which includes unpublished, out-of-print and new writing about art, both serious and playful (from *Degas and his Model* and *On Contemporary Art* to *Pissing Figures: 1280–2014* and *Thrust: A Spasmodic Pictorial History of the Codpiece in Art*), an assortment of slim volumes designed to slip easily into a tote or pocket and carry along anywhere, with covers as mesmerizing as the rocks and minerals section of a natural history museum – one might be sulfurous, another malachite, amethyst, ochre, ruby, aquamarine, rose quartz, citrine, lapis lazuli.

Historically, ekphrasis was a term used to describe any vivid depiction in words, though it has come to mean more specifically a description of artwork in writing. There is a long tradition of rendering a painting, sculpture or architecture into poetic language. One of the first known examples, the fourth-century rhetorician Aphthonius's *Progymnasmata*, was a textbook of sorts, filled with training exercises (*Common topic: Against a tyrant... Characterization: What Niobe would say on the death of her children... Description: The temple in Alexandria, together with the acropolis... Thesis: Should one marry?*). This was considered an important way to learn how to write well into the Renaissance, where the notion of *ut pictura poesis* loosely translates 'as is painting so is poetry'.

Instances of ekphrastic poetry are as varied as they are plentiful: Homer's shield of Achilles influenced Hesoid's shield of Herakles; there is Sappho's temple of Aphrodite; the ivory cup given by the goatherd to the shepherd Thyrsis in Theocritus's *Idylls*; the armour of Aeneas in

Virgil's *Aeneid*; the relief sculptures in Dante's *Purgatorio*; the tapestries and frescoes in Ariosto and Spencer; Catullus 64; Shakespeare's *The Rape of Lucrece*; Shelley's 'On the Medusa of Leonardo Da Vinci in the Florentine Gallery'; Keats's 'Ode on a Grecian Urn' and 'On Seeing the Elgin Marbles'; Robert Browning's 'My Last Duchess'; Elizabeth Barrett Browning's 'On a Portrait of Wordsworth, by R.B. Haydon'; Hope Mirrlees's 'A Meditation on Donatello's Annunciation in the Church of Santa Croce, Florence'; Auden's 'Musée des Beaux Arts'; William Carlos Williams's 'Landscape with the Fall of Icarus'; Mina Loy's 'Brancusi's Golden Bird' and 'Stravinski's Flute'; Marianne Moore's 'An Egyptian Pulled Glass Bottle in the Shape of a Fish'; Tomas Tranströmer's 'The Palace'; Rita Dove's 'Agosta the Winged Man and Rasha the Black Dove'; Brigit Pegeen Kelly's 'Garden of Flesh, Garden of Stone':

> lengths of blue, lengths of gray,
> yards and yards of quarried white. And the boy,
> who is made of stone, who has stood still for a long time,
> pissing in the stone basin...

In Tolstoy's *Anna Karenina*, both Mikhailov and Vronsky paint Anna's portrait, though Vronsky abandons his version; in Austen's *Emma*, Emma paints Harriet's portrait while Mr. Elton lurks nearby; in Charlotte Brontë's *Villette*, Lucy Snowe describes a painting of Cleopatra in a gallery – 'that wealth of muscle, that affluence of flesh' – before Monsieur Paul Emanuel chastises and directs her to more appropriate artwork (that is, in Snowe's words, 'flat, dead, pale, and formal'). In Fleur Jaeggy's *I Am the Brother of XX*, nymphs that are 'wet, rapacious' walk in and out of paintings in a museum, Venus is uncrated and takes a breath, a portrait of an unknown woman becomes a thief.

Some of Karl Ove Knausgård's most responsive, acutely felt moments in the *My Struggle* series move in and around art:

> ... the moment I focused my gaze on the picture again all my reasoning vanished in the surge of energy and beauty that arose in me. *Yes, yes, yes*, I heard. *That's where it is. That's where I have to go.*
> (from *A Death in the Family*)

Whether referring to Rembrandt, Turner, Caravaggio, Vermeer, Constable, Balke, Dürer, Ernst, Munch, Blake's *Newton* painting, drawings from Churchill's eighteenth-century expedition or a cabinet of curiosities, Knausgård brings them into the immediate moment, giving them modern-day relevance, a past that tethers to the present and back, a timelessness that is reassuring, connecting thoughts and ideas, feeling and understanding. Not merely a description of a work of art but what one might bring to the experience of viewing it, stirring up what has perhaps been in stasis.

For this is what ekphrasis can do, a *mise-en-abyme*-like variation of a variation that reveals the vivacity of beauty and the gruesome lack thereof, an otherworldly window into vulnerabilities and needs, a verbal representation of the visual that motions the reader into new experiential places and reverberates around the senses, as palpable as eating a lemon macaron in Le Marais or noticing the metallic air just before a rainstorm.

'The power of art to harmonize the self with itself and with the world', writes Vernon Lee in *The Psychology of an Art Writer*. Born Violet Paget in 1856, Lee observed the physical sensations of looking at art, the effects on the body of the beholder, how 'the silvery sheen of an olive tree, the *dove-dappled-gray* colour of a lake' might be taken in, processed and re-expressed into words, how one might feel euphoric or irritated or indifferent depending on one's mood while studying Signorelli's *Last Judgement*, Titian's *Assumption*, statues by Sansovino and Canova, Botticelli in the Uffizi Gallery, a Sabine priestess at the Loggia dei Lanzi, Melpomene holding the mask of Hercules, one version at the Louvre, another at the Vatican Museum.

Sometimes Lee is 'tired, bored, disinclined to look at anything', at others she has 'strong palpitations, a general sense of cat's fur brushed the wrong way'. Sometimes there is a bubbling up of pleasure, other times a great sigh of relief, the body's sudden satisfying decompression. Contemplating *Portrait of Innocent X* by Velázquez, she notices the chair and sitter askew, so 'that we should feel, *as he does, the other unseen side...*'.

The direction of the gaze, the impression of planes in detail, suggestion of movement and gesture, existence in space, a sense of *aliveness* and feeling, something real to hold onto, are important to Lee, as is colour – 'cold rose, warm grey, vivid geranium', 'pleasure, in a very deep sea-green Perugino background', also '[c]ertain blues and lilacs catch me at once with a sense of bodily rapture, unlocalised but akin to that of tastes and smells. Also certain qualities of flesh, its firmness, warmth...'.

To taste a shade of violet, smell a sunlit yellow. In these synesthesia-like flashes, a transference occurs: 'I then begin to see the relief, go *into* the picture...' she writes of Baldovinetti's *Madonna and Saints*. For some, art can be a sensory experience that slips around the pleasure centres of the mind, all-encompassing, insistent, transformative. 'The work of art is the joint product', she continues, 'the point of intersection of the process of the attention of the artist who makes it (hence Löwy's *memory images*, etc.), and of the process of attention of those who look at it'.

In photographs for exhibits of Ruth Asawa's wire sculptures, for instance, I see droplets of water gliding down a windowless window, cells dividing, dendrites, mitochondria, viruses, nerve-endings, the fins of a fish, amoeba-like entities, organisms alive and amorphous and breathing. There is airiness, a sense of floating, of expansiveness and possibility, of uncontained containment. Vivian Suter's brightly coloured canvases hanging unframed and overlapping on the walls and from the ceiling in the middle of a gallery, free to waver and curl, drape and overlap, are compelling emotional affairs, a chattering of conversations, playful and joyous and crisp at times, at times moody and aphotic and weathered, a leaf caught in the paint, a wavelike image whipped by the wind.

'The total impression of a work of art is, I think, the sum of a series of acts of attention', Lee surmises. This need for concentration, focus and discipline are reaffirmed in Rilke's *Letters to a Young Painter* when he addresses the young Balthus: 'There you have it, my dear. Try, make an effort, there is nothing in life that doesn't produce a very valuable and ultimately individual pleasure if only we are a little persistent'.

'My dear Balthus, *bon courage!*' Rilke repeats, the way Rodin used to offer *bon courage* to Rilke. He often followed his mentor's advice ('you must work, always work', Rodin had determined, in order to dedicate one's life to art without distraction). In writing his *Letters to a Young Poet,* Rilke moves no less than seven times, from Paris to Pisa to Bremen to Rome to cities in Sweden and back to Paris; in *Letters to a Young Painter* four times, from a castle in Zurich to a château in Valais to Vaud back to the château in Valais, in search of rest, good health, the space to think and write.

It was after leaving his wife and daughter in Germany to live in Paris for six years that he reconnected with close friend and artist Baladine Klossowska, after she separated from her husband, along with her children Pierre and Balthus, and they lived together as a family – with a stray cat named Mitsou. Klossowska and her children would eventually move to Berlin without Rilke, who had isolated himself in a state of ecstatic rapture while writing the *Duino Elegies* (from 'The Second Elegy': 'But we, when moved by deep feeling, evaporate; we / breathe ourselves out and away...') and *Sonnets to Orpheus* ('But out of listening. Bellow, cry, and roar...').

Letters to a Young Painter has a distinct feel from *Letters to a Young Poet*. Rather than the 'nobody can counsel and help you, nobody' and 'we are unutterably alone' tone of the poet-letters (signed 'Ever yours: Rainer Maria Rilke'), the painter-letters, written twenty years later, are lighter, breezier, more affectionate and encouraging, a merging between father figure, friend and fellow artist. He recounts a story about a gap that forms at midnight:

> between the day that was ending and the one about to begin, and that a very nimble and clever person who managed to slip into that gap would escape from time and find himself in a realm free of all the changes we are subject to. All the things we have lost are gathered there – Mitsou, for example... broken dolls from childhood, etc., etc.

He cautions Balthus, though, to peer into that space rather than leap right in. Later, he sends his love 'as though I were still the / Réne of the old days'. (Born Réne, he changed his name to Rainer at the suggestion of a former lover, Lou Andreas-Salomé, who considered it stronger, more Germanic, then changed it back to the French-sounding Réne.)

The letters offer glimpses into Rilke and (through Rilke) Balthus's day-to-day, most of the letters written near Balthus's 'invisible' leap-year birthday on February 29. Interests and ideas that inform both of their arts practices are captured in a caring, easygoing manner – a Middle Ages exhibition at the Bibliothèque Nationale ('it must be astonishing!'); the seventeenth-century drawings of flowers and animals at the Pavillon Marsan; the magnificent Cedar of Lebanon that adorns the Jardin des Plantes brought as a sapling in the crown of botanist Le Jussieau's hat in 1734; the issue of Válery's 'Notes on Narcissus' from the 12-volume *Série de L'Horloge*; a water-colour of Rilke's parents painted by Klossowska; the copy of Nicolas Poussin's *Echo and Narcissus* that Balthus paints for Rilke. Rilke's poem 'Narcissus', in turn, is dedicated to Balthus ('It's the return of all desire that enters / toward all life embracing itself from afar...').

And then there is the missing Mitsou, adored by Balthus, inspiration for the charmingly dramatic thick-lined drawings in *Mitsou: Forty Images by Baltusz*, to which Rilke writes the preface: 'Can one lose a cat, a living thing, a living being, a life? To lose a life is death! / Well, then, it's death'.

Cats continue to wander in and out of their lives, in Rilke's poem 'Black Cat' – 'A ghost, though invisible, still is like a place / your sight can knock on, echoing...', and many more in Balthus's paintings, including *Le Chat de la Méditérranée* (1949), *Le Roi des Chats* (1935), *La Patience* (1943), *Le Chat au miroir I, II and III* (1980, 1986, 1989), the *Thérèse* paintings (1938–1939) and *Jeune fille à la mandolin* (2000–2001), lapping milk from a saucer, rubbing up against the artist's legs, slipping out from around a corner, sitting on a chair, taking the shape of a human. Klossowska, too, would paint a watercolour of Balthus's arms around a tabby; her two children seated at an addled table set with striped tablecloth, pale-blue napkins, a splash of green, pears perhaps; Rilke resting on a sofa (*La Contemplation Intérieure: Rilke dormant sur un petit sofa à Muzot*, 1921).

Rilke was well aware of connection and influence, faith and the desire to create, the need to be alone, to press an ear against an invisible wall and wait as long as necessary for the words to come. In his second to last letter to Balthus, dated 24 February, 1926, ten months before his death, Rilke writes about 'the harmony being created between your imagination and everything that happens to you', which Balthus would echo decades later: 'All of a sudden the vision that pre-existed incarnates itself, more or less intuitively and more or less precisely. The dream and the reality are superimposed and made one'.

For H.D., artistic expression was an aqueous cap: 'transparent, fluid yet with definite body... like a closed sea-plant, jelly-fish or anemone', something she called the over-mind, where 'thoughts pass and are visible like fish swimming under clear water', or like a lens, where 'the whole world of vision is open to us'.

The essays in *Visions and Ecstasies*, many published for the first time, are filled with other intriguing, manifesto-like statements and perceptions:

Most of the so-called artists of today have lost the use of their brain.

We begin with sympathy of thought.

The minds of the two lovers merge, interact in sympathy of thought.

There is no trouble about art, it is the appreciators we want.

If you cannot be entertained and instructed by Boccaccio, Rabelais, Montaigne, Sterne, Middleton, de Gourmont and de Régnier there is something wrong with you physically.

There is plenty of pornographic literature that is interesting and amusing.

There is nothing horrible in the statues of gods, half-gods, maidens and winged deities of the Acropolis...

Headstrong and demonstrative, H.D is remembered predominantly for her Imagist poetry, a movement that has always confined her reputation, as movements and categories are wont to do, especially if one doesn't quite fit in. (Another H.D. statement: 'The new schools of destructive art theorists are on the wrong track'.)

Filled with images of the sea and flowers – roses, violets, rhododendrons, irises, poppies, hyacinths, crocuses and hepaticas that appear to be just that, roses, violets, Rhododendrons, irises, poppies, hyacinths, crocuses and hepaticas – her language teeters toward the overly tender:

My mouth is wet with your life,
my eyes blinded by your face,
a heart itself which feels
the intimate music...
    (from the poem 'Eros')

Yet one cannot help but appreciate the desire to recreate the garden of Dionysus, with its 'fragrant wild azalea and wild rose-tree brush', its honeysuckle and myrtle, a place where the crocuses are 'walled against blue of themselves' and saffron have 'very golden hearts'. Who wouldn't want to sit in such a garden, its efflorescence offering both beauty and decay, insights and, as in the Jardin des Plantes, *les carrés de la perspective*:

At least I have the flowers of myself,
and my thoughts, no god
can take that;
I have the fervour of myself for a presence
and my own spirit for light...
    (from 'Eurydice')

In other tropistic instances, ideas and syntax bend and turn in the most engaging ways. Take 'Toward the Piraeus':

If I had been a boy,
I would have worshipped your grace,
I would have flung my worship
before your feet,

I would have followed apart,
glad, rent with an ecstasy
to watch you turn
your great head, set on the throat,
thick, dark with its sinews,
burned and wrought
like the olive stalk,
and the noble chin
and the throat.

I would have stood,
and watched and watched
and burned...

In short essays 'Notes on Thought and Vision', 'People of Sparta', 'From Megara to Corinth', 'A Poet in the Wilderness: Songs of Anacreon' and 'Curled Thyme', H.D. continues to explore gender, sexuality and the artistic process, incorporating flowers and Greek mythology into her writing, likening Euripides to a white rose, 'lyric, feminine, a spirit'. She talks about the Eleusinian Mysteries, 'coloured marbles and brown pottery, painted with red and vermillion...', and its three phases – the descent, the search, the ascent – as the three stages of creative awareness. The *Charioteer of Delphi* – 'the bend of his arm, the knife-cut of his chin... the fall of his drapery, in geometric precision' – not created by 'inspiration', but 'sheer, hard brain work'.

She goes on to posit the ideas of the body as an oyster, the soul a pearl, the womb as a space of creativity, and wonders if a man's 'love-region' compares to that of a female's, associating the creation of art to giving birth. In a similar manner, images of wombs and foetuses appear in many of Frida Kahlo's paintings – in *Moses*, or *Nucleus of Creation* (1945), a womb rains tears; in *Henry Ford Hospital* (1932) the womb is a broken jacaranda-like flower tied to a red string; in *Without Hope* (1945) internal organs spew forth from her mouth; in *My Birth* (1932) she pushes her own bloodied head out from between her legs – so many struggles to conceive. In the poem 'Parturition', the painter and poet Mina Loy speaks of '[t]he contents of the universe' made in and by her own body – a human being, a painting, a piece of writing:

Repose
Which never comes.
For another mountain is growing up
Which   goaded by the unavoidable
I must traverse
Traversing myself...

According to H.D., 'it was before the birth of my child that the jelly-fish consciousness seemed to come definitely in to the field or realm of the intellect or brain', and a wealth of poetry and prose soon followed – not only *Notes on Thought and Vision* (1919) but *Paint It Today* (1919), *Translations* (1920), *Hymen* (1921) and *Heliodora and Other Poems* (1924). In the novel *Asphodel* (written in 1921 but not published until 1992), the main character, Hermione, travels on a boat from New York to France ('Stairs in her imagination heaved and sank under her. She seemed about to float away, lax, bodiless...'), where,

seasick, disembodied, a voice repeats 'There is nothing wrong with you' three times before she realizes: '... de Maupassant was true. Literature was true. If de Maupassant was true then life and letters met, were not subdivided, hermetically shut apart. *Helen thy beauty is to me...*'. Helen, Zeus, Hesperus, Calypso, Odysseus, Sappho – they open their arms and mouths, breathe and battle, leap from page to page, from poem to novel to essay. As for admired artists such as Leonardo da Vinci, H.D. supposes '[he] saw the faces of many of his youths and babies and young women definitely in his over-mind', that 'his kind are never old, never dead', that creation of any sort requires a convergence of consciousness, skill, conviction, and perhaps most important of all, devotion. If a painting such as *Madonna of the Rocks* is not a picture but a window, as H.D. suggests, then one must actively and diligently take the time to look through in order to truly see.

In the translator's note to *Chardin and Rembrandt*, Jennie Feldman writes that 'the leap between art and life is a dynamic one' and that '[ar]rt is the spur to an imaginative exploration of the inner worlds of others', ultimately an exploration of one's own inner world, with so many worries and fantasies, memories and emotions milling about.

Written by Proust, *Chardin and Rembrandt* is perhaps the most exciting of the ekphrasis series, an unfinished essay (twenty years before the writing of the seven-volume *In Search of Lost Time / Remembrance of Things Past*) that ends midsentence, and even in its incompleteness reveals the progression of images and ideas that would lead to his most ambitious and celebrated work, where, after dipping a now-clichéd madeleine into lime-blossom tea, Marcel sees in exceptional detail his life before him, 'the glimmering flame of the night-light in its bowl of Bohemian glass' and 'the chimney-piece of Siena marble' in his bedroom at Combray, the V-shaped opening of Mlle Vinteuil's crepe bodice and the depth of a blue-violet pond that suggests 'a floor of Japanese cloisonné', 'the kings of chivalry with lilies in their hands' and a 'bloom of light' that characterizes 'certain passages of *Lohengrin*, certain paintings by Carpaccio', the Angel's trumpet in 'The Dance of Death' by Baudelaire, all of which reveal 'a wink of connivance, a hint, a sudden meaning, a secret understanding, all the mysteries of complicity in a plot...'.

(Proust would go on to write about Chardin, in Volume III, *The Guermantes Way*, for example, where the painter M. Elstir is an admirer of his paintings: 'Elstir sought to wrest from what he had just felt what he already knew; he had often been at pains to break up that medley of impressions which we call vision.')

The start of the essay imagines an unnamed young man, bored after the midday meal, gazing at the unruly table, which bothers him less than the neatness to be found in the rest of the room. He leaves his domestic ennui, and his mother sewing – not to mention the dishes on the table, lucky him – by going to the Louvre 'in search of Veronese's palaces, Van Dyck's princes, Claude Lorrain's harbours'.

It is here that the narrator peeks into a doorway, breaking through a wall: 'I would not put him off going to the

Louvre – indeed, I would accompany him', leading the young man through the La Caze room and the gallery of eighteenth-century French painters to get to the works of Chardin.

Chardin's still lifes have always been more alive than still. In the colour plates that accompany the text – which include *The Diligent Mother*; *The Buffet*; *Kitchen Utensils, Cauldron, Saucepan, and Eggs*; *The Ray* – one can see the scenes of domesticity the young man has tried desperately to escape – a shiny copper saucepan, a clutch of eggs, a pyramid of glistening plums and peaches, creased white table linen. Proust's language is evocative and memorable, from the extraordinary description of a cut-open ray's 'vast and delicate architecture, tinted with red blood, blue nerves, and white muscle, like the nave of a polychrome church', to '[o]ysters as light as cupped mother-of-pearl and as cool as the seawater', and dead fish in 'stiff, desperate arcs, flat on their bellies, eyes bulging'. A self-portrait of Chardin, complete with eyeshade and peach-coloured scarf wrapped around his head and knotted at the neck, reminds Proust of an elderly woman, an English tourist, someone eccentric (this was the 1890s), but Chardin was able to capture the way he saw himself, or needed to, in soft light, wrapped in silks, Stygian shadows in the background.

Proust's talk about Rembrandt, meanwhile, throws open the rest of the windows. In *The Philosopher in Meditation* there is 'the glaze and glitter of blazing windows', 'how the light reddens a window like a furnace or paints it like stained glass', which, in Proust's mind, is 'the gleam borrowed from beauty, the divine gaze'.

Soon after, the essay stops short, never fully realized, but with illuminating conclusions along the way: 'We have learned that a pear is as alive as a woman, a plain earthenware vessel as beautiful as a precious stone'. That art has the ability to revel in the beauty of the everyday, what is perhaps glazed over, dismissed, diminished, taken for granted, unfinished; it 'addresses our life, comes to touch upon it, slowly inclining us towards things ... bringing us closer to the heart of them'.

There are many other sides unseen, of course. In *Thrust: A Spasmodic Pictorial History of the Codpiece in Art* Michael Glover humorously recounts the history of the codpiece, from Titian, where 'a mighty phallus was an object of wonder', to Pieter Bruegel the Elder's *The Wedding Dance* (1566), where merry men think it no trouble to point themselves every which way, and Giorgione's *The Tempest*, where a mother nurses her baby while a well-endowed fellow in tight embroidered breeches watches. One accoutrement might appear as though a snail's shell between the legs, another 'shoots up curvaceously, like a rearing horse', a gearshift, overripe fruit hanging from a branch. In Wilde's *The Critic As Artist*,

Ernest and Gilbert banter back and forth all night:

Gilbert: All art is immoral.
Ernest: All art?
Gilbert: Yes.

until '[a] faint purple mist hangs over the Park, and the shadows of the white houses are purple', and they decide to go to Covent Garden to gaze at the roses.

In times of great uncertainty and worry, one turns to art for consolation, escape, recognition, determination, different vantages, what Proust calls 'a sharper awareness', a voice for what is silent, an entrance into another space, a meaningful exchange. I might imagine, then, the radiant lapis lazuli that highlights the heavens like water in Giotto's frescoes, how Ruskin, in *Giotto and His Works in Padua*, spoke of '[Giotto's] love of what was most mysterious, yet most comforting and full of hope', how in *Swann's Way* Proust talks about the time it took Marcel to appreciate and understand 'Charity devoid of charity', and Knausgård, in *A Death in the Family*, of 'the aura of vulnerability' in people's eyes. I might imagine seeing a version of Artemisia Gentileschi's *Judith Slaying Holofernes* (1620–1621) at the Uffizi, a spray of blood like a burst pipe, Judith's dress, the colour of cobalt at the Museo Capodimonte, now golden, blood-splattered, revealing; how in *Self-portrait as the Allegory of Painting* (1638–1639) the canvas she paints remains blank; the first major exhibition of her work, *Artemisia*, at the National Gallery postponed until further notice. I might imagine walking through the marbled corridors of the Louvre, past Géricault's *The Raft of the Medusa*, through Room 17 to visit the Roman copies of the *Three Graces* (circle around them and one can see a scattering of timeworn bruises on their backs), *Capitoline Venus* standing after a bath, the perfectly tranquil *Sleeping Hermaphroditus*, then up the staircase to the Denon wing, where *Winged Victory of Samothrace* prepares for eternal flight.

Notes

The Psychology of an Art Writer by Vernon Lee, translated by Jeff Nagy (2018) £8.95
Letters to a Young Painter by Rainer Maria Rilke, translated by Damion Searls (2017) £8.95
Visions and Ecstasies by H.D. (2019) £8.95
Chardin and Rembrandt by Marcel Proust, translated by Jennie Feldman (2016) £8.95
Thrust: A Spasmodic Pictorial History of the Codpiece in Art by Michael Glover (2019) £8.95
The Critic As Artist by Oscar Wilde (2019) £8.95
Giotto and His Works in Padua by John Ruskin (2018) £8.95

Empire

JOHN GREENING

for Jane

They climb the stairs of our little house,
those black-and-white pictures of your father
escorting the Sultan of Zanzibar, who's

in robes and headdress, bearded, bent,
to the inevitable. None of your mother,
though she was the heart of government

and ruled your waves when I invaded
Hampton's post-imperial maze,
toxic twists and turns and dead

ends baffling to a boy from the Heath.
Here, Geoffrey's standing at ease
in his white uniform, beneath

the coconut palm, with two judges,
a general, the medals, the gowns.
Nothing is going to change. He marches

ahead of the Sultan watched by troops
who've shouldered arms on the trim lawns
and know what's out of shot. At the top

stair it simply ends, though there's
a haughty portrait of a WAAF – that's Anne,
around the time they met, some years

before the Colonial Course and Dar,
when you were no more thought of than decline
and fall, just after the war.

*

What right did they have? Had Africa
invited them in to set it straight?
Not something I would ever dare

raise when your mother and father were living,
not even over a drink, since that
was how it began. Soon to be leaving

ourselves (neo-colonialists,
or so a friend of your father quipped)
for Egypt. But the question persists

for those outside the private hedges,
those like me, bred to be kept
behind privet: were the privileges

of house and garden, club and car,
drinks, and spice-encrusted foods,
health and wealth, casual power,

excused by what that power achieved,
the pipes, the wires, the rails, the roads,
the good they did? I almost believed.

*

If they didn't know their new start
was only the start of the final act,
perhaps it's because they knew it hurt

to look hard at the sun – though being
dazzled breeds a kind of respect
for lofty gilded whiteness. Knowing

at Bagamoya in Livingstone's house
(two years before you arrived)
that the ground floor had once been used

for slaves, did they never feel
living where those traders lived
was too close to be comfortable?

To swampy Kilosa, to Morogoro,
then Dar again, building schools
(to instil, the cynic says, a thorough

appreciation of sweetness and light
and how to obey the British rules)
Jane Sarah Anne not yet

– but soon – smearing melony fingers
across her Daddy D.O's plans
at making the law stick, to bring

as fair a regime as any imperial
enterprise since Rome, to Mwanza
and keep the centuries-old colonial

cogs (all made in England) oiled
and turning, with essence of class and race.
The band struck up, but no one smiled,

as Zanzibar hove into view
and a family stepped down, with, yes
a child at last. That would be you.

*

Arab and African shield their eyes,
the giant tortoise hides in its shell,
colonies within colonies.

Forget it for the scent of cloves ,
the sound of coconuts as they fall
beside you. Everyone loves

a new child, who breathes the scent
and hears the fall, and is handed to
an ayah. Hear that strange lament,

Swahili lullaby, do you
remember it? No, no,
the words you took to heart and knew

have gone, but if the music played...?
You toddle on the coral shore
innocent, naked, unafraid

of anything the Indian Ocean
might be warning, and ignore
the undercurrent, revolution.

*

It's barely possible to admit
still less explain these days those seven
years you grew on the edge of white

mischief: delight and joy, the glory
of an island to yourself, a haven
to snorkel in, a palmy shore

to walk bare-footed, your soles
forever rough and hard from when
you trod coral. Everything spoils

dumped along the Uxbridge Road
or squeezed on to the Fulwell train
but that's the future. Your father strode

beside the Sultan faithfully
as the sun began to set, toward
the sixties, private secretary

glimpsed in the frame of a Pathé clip
on YouTube, a lovingly Word-
Pressed memoir, or in the sleep

of this younger District Officer
at a nursing home on the Sussex coast:
'Woodland? Geoffrey... if he's the...

unless it's the chap I dreamt I knew
who stared out the moon, cried that the feast
might begin... last night.' But who

sees Colonial as anything other
than a hollow conch, a dress sword
on the wall, that Arab chest your father

and mother kept in Hampton? And what
it contained, who knows? I heard
funeral music in the topee, but not

a clue was breathed from the chest. A history
of the British Empire, maybe, bound
in leather, silver? With a mystery

or two – the tale of how a small
and insignificant island found
a way to make its part the whole.

*

A young man climbs the palm
barefoot, in his hand a machete.
A rustle, a slither, and down, slam

to the ground, to a fresh green heap
and the old woman. Much later,
she'll sit at her *mbuzi* and grip

a brown husk (you're watching and listening),
pound it steadily, scrape the white
interior, beat its damp and glistening

flesh to fragments, which she will use
for what, your ayah? Ah, that
nameless love, as you're in Waitrose

walking the freezing aisles: it moves
among packets of desiccated
coconut, and dried cloves.

The Father Heavens

JOE CARRICK-VARTY

After Buddhism at the British Library, 25 October 2019 – 29 February 2020

Father Cosmology

This cosmological map depicts the heavenly
realm called 82a Wytham Street with palaces, gardens
and marketplaces for the 33 fathers who reside there.
In the middle is the settee of the father
Daniel who is lord of this heaven. See
the hot rock hole, the ancient shape of a backside.
Take a seat. Oh, you've done that before. This is one
of six heavens or celestial realms.

Great Peacock Wisdom King

This manual contains paintings of altars for
sons who will one day become fathers
and may end up alone in a flat or may not.
One father can be seen riding a peacock, a bird that
keeps a territory free from snakes. Can you spot
the note left three years ago saying *I've hoovered*?
Yes, a faint smell of skin and Hula Hoops. On the right
a father appears in a stylised wheel. Between
the spokes are the names for certain kinds of shadow.

Fathers of Previous World Cycles

In the Theravāda tradition, four fathers are believed
to have attained Nirvana. The history of these fathers
is given in a text which is traditionally read
to sons in the bath. Kukusandha father
(top) is the first father, Konāgamana is the second
father, Kassapa is the third father and the
historical father Daniel born as Our Prince Danny
is the fourth and final father of this era. Every
father has always achieved enlightenment
in the shadow of a certain tree.

Life Father

Fatherhood is described as a series of manifestations
that are impermanent. It is thought that there
is no ultimate reality in things – every father
is subject to change and to some extent
dependent (dep / en / dent) on perception.
Sonhood does not encourage
belief in a creator deity or
supreme being. However, where
have you walked to this Sunday morning?
Get up from this settee. Close that empty fridge.
See the years of letters at the door?
Gather them up.

Palinodes in the Voice of My Dead Father

JEE LEONG KOH

'A palinode or palinody is an ode in which the writer retracts a view or sentiment expressed in an earlier poem. The first recorded use of a palinode is in a poem by Stesichorus in the 7th century B.C., in which he retracts his earlier statement that the Trojan War was all the fault of Helen.' (Wikipedia)

Palinode I

Your mom, look
at her, crying

so piteously,
as my body is

wheeled
into the fire.

There she goes,
collapsing

into herself,
like a burning roof.

Hold her up.
Hold her

close, my
Hecuba.

I'm sorry I
ever thought

of her
as Helen.

Palinode III

All the time
the air sacs

in my lungs
winked out

like lights
in an inhabited

valley,
the locks

of my heart
closed

at semi-regular
intervals,

my legs
waterlogged,

I thought,
I have no regrets

for living
the way I did, where I did.

The lights
blessed

the smoky Saturday dances
with the

implausibly
slim waists

of girls.
The canals met

us with boats
on their leisured

way
somewhere

to which our legs
would deliver us.

But we never
left the valley.

We bought a house,
paid for

by running
the machines maintaining

cool and comfortable
the valley air.

We had the two
of you,

as the valley said
to do.

And then, first,
the smog drifted

over
from the next valley

and choked to death
all our animals

and the smog,
staying years and years,

so long we had almost
acclimatized ourselves to it,

was followed
by the flood.

Palinode VII

I met a suicide
here,

a young man
who looked

eighteen,
who could not

stop talking
in parables.

He had made
the world

a better place,
he was convinced,

by leaving it,
but, boy,

how he missed,
how he missed,

his friend
who was more than a friend.

Palinode VIII

At the cinema
you were

excited by the bare-bodied
students

of kung fu
lifting water buckets

on their broad
shoulders,

the Hollywood
car chase

led by an amnesiac
Marine captain

at the flashing wheel,
and so was I,

looking for a shot
of testosterone

in
my disabled life,

until the picture
of you

taken from behind
came unbidden

on the screen,
and I

had to close my eyes
against

the fire engulfing
the overturned

car, the water buckets
clattering

down
the temple steps.

Palinode XVII

The rat
that leapt off

my back
to enter heaven

first
is still a rat.

I am an ox,
stoic and traditional,

keeping
to the rich furrows

cut by
abiding love.

It's true:
when I was ten

I wished
I were a monkey,

overturning heaven
with my

antics, changing
into a fish,

a freckled bustard,
a roadside

shrine.
But mother died

and went ahead
of me

and all wishes for change
left too.

If I should turn
into

a rooster or a pig,
how would

she recognize her boy
when she

passed by the rocky
fields?

Or, now,
these regions of fire?

Essaying On...

KIRSTY GUNN

I have been keeping time to a sort of music in these pages recently. Writing first about exploring new ways of critical and poetic thinking in a beautiful Georgian room formerly given over to string quartets and a grand piano, and now of the activities circling around that composition, many and various yet in happy counterpoint to the original theme of risk, attempt and the give-it-a-go *essayer* that is the key note of essay form.

For essays are not just a way of writing about thinking, I am coming to realise, but a whole way of being in the world. They help us imagine and describe reality, discover fresh means of expression. They are not only part of that 'adventure into language' as Seamus Heaney, in his Nobel Prize Acceptance speech, described his own life's work but are also a portal through which one can view one's thinking, writing self. Essays are not just for essayists, then; they're good for all of us. In that same speech Heaney talks about 'the temple inside my hearing', the place in the mind that is alert to and representative of the effect of poetry, and so it does now seem to me as though that kind of 'listening' might be applied as well to the circling patterns of thought around the short stories and poems that we make as it does to essays drawn from the world around us. Both require a fine tuning of words to discover the sensibility beneath – to give to our mute, aphonic selves music.

And such pleasure there is to be had in this coming into voice! For as I've been saying to students – not just at Merton College where I have been talking about essaying recently[1] but in Scotland, too, and London, where a number of different essaying projects have also been initiated – there is a great feeling of freedom in this form. An essay is outward facing and expansive; it makes space for new forms of creativity. It allows for other disciplines and art forms – poetry, drawing, painting, biography, as well as history, science, mathematics – and is not closed off to yet more ideas arriving within its pages, right up to the very last sentence. It's a freedom we need to exercise. For in these constrained and perverted post-truth times, of pandemic and lock down, of untrustworthy politicians and advisers, how important it is to show young people a language that speaks so differently from the bullish diction of our age, where the lies of 'I believe' and 'I am certain' rankly outnumber the hesitancies of ethics and philosophy. Essays give students a 'space' where their enquiring minds may be given full rein. When universities have let their teaching programmes be so constrained by aims and outcomes and so-called 'Quality Monitoring' metrics, essays feel enabling; here is a form of writing that lets all kinds of thinking out into the open air.

This is not to say, of course, I remind the students, that one simply picks up a pen and follows the line of one's thoughts – although indeed we do exactly that in our round table sessions together, whether in the beautiful room in Oxford or in seminar sessions at Dundee. Because it is, most certainly, the case that when, after setting down a poem before them, along with a prompt (a flower, perhaps, or fruit, a line of text; that 'temple inside my hearing' from Heaney, again, would be perfect here) there are only a couple of minutes given them to read and consider before they're off! And for sure, picking up pens and paper and letting them hit the page in a single timed shot – I make it about ten minutes, with time taken later to edit and cut or add further material – is a fabulously exciting way of catching the flight of a thought as it's released from the reading and exercise that have been set, no doubt about that. But letting the pen on the paper track those winging responses is 'first draft thinking' only. Essays must come beautifully finished and edited when they are finally presented for reading or assessment; as with all good writing they are... refined.

So we must take up the 'scarves of our drafts' – as I've been calling these first attempts at thinking, pages, I am hoping, of scribbled lines and ideas and the random and various associations collected around these tracks of thoughts un-stoppered from our minds – and lay them down on the table, smoothing out the edges and going into them now to *work* on them, to flense off the parts we don't need, to add fresh lines to those areas of the text that need extra presence, a deepening of intellectual questioning, or the glitter of metaphor to make a certain point show itself, to concentrate a quote or an image... We labour then, to overhaul a paragraph here, re-calibrate the meaning of a reference there. We must pay attention, I say, to what our writing wants to say – so that we can let meaning emerge from all the words we've first put down in that first great rush of response and imagination as though crisp and fresh as a newly minted thought. 'Drafting' I remind them, 'rewriting, writing in, writing over, writing through...', showing them the meticulous work of essayist Chris Arthur and his reminder taken form Basho: 'Let there not be a hair's breadth separating your mind from what you write...' This is also what essaying is all about.

As though to reflect this process and celebrate it, my sister the painter Merran Gunn has created a set of these 'scarves' or banners for the Music Room in Oxford: thin hangings of rice paper stained and dyed, and in chalks and inks the lines of various bits of writing appear through the soaked colours... 'memories that will shape images not yet conceived...', I read, and 'to renounce control... willingly, consciously...', and 'these fragments remain...'. So we see how essays can become artworks, performances of a kind; here on parchments that hang tentatively from a wall and flutter in an unexpected breeze. They don't need to serve some function or other. Essays don't have to tell or to explain – although they may well be put to use in all kinds of surprising ways. In the first instance, though, as with a poem, an essay can simply... be.

The 'creative writing workshop', that idea founded in post war America, as a kind of intervention of state – to return servicemen and women, after the years of aimless combat and national action, to a sense of work and imperative by providing a 'creative' method by which to re enter society – is not a useful idea for those of us keen on essaying about the place. That word 'workshop', even, with its associations of sweatshop and the industrial line – not to mention various dubious notions around 'permission' and 'me-time' that seem to inhabit the very phrase 'creative writing', as if all writing were not creative, anyhow... – these and more are reasons why publishing historian and founder of the poetry review magazine DURA, Gail Low, and I call what we do 'Creative Essaying'. These teaching sessions that are not so much lectures as talks, shared by the two of us, in a lecture room arranged with large tables that we can sit down and move around, are as intent upon reading as they are on writing. Essaying has become an attractive way to bind the two together, we've found, keeping the texts close at hand as discussion and the writing exercises develop and we encourage students to read aloud or pin their fragments and ideas and reactions to their reading upon the wall for us all to see.

The idea first to range about, somewhat, listening, wondering, and then finally to catch and mount seems to me to capture in one this 'essaying' initiative of ours. Students have been knocked into submission by what they've been told an essay is, so we've noticed: A tame creature indeed that plods down the page in a 'five paragraph' set as the recent *Why They Can't Write* by John Warner, just published by Johns Hopkins Press, attests. If the teaching room is a place of 'complexity', a 'subtle topology of corporeal relations, of which knowledge is only the *pre-text...*', as Roland Barthes outlined it, so imaginatively and provocatively in his own essay 'To the Seminar', then our young people seem to have had little experience of it in their high schools and undergraduate 'pathways' where learning is all focused upon grades and teaching is engineered so as to achieve them. No wonder our cry to 'Just Write' brings a ripple of panic into most rooms. Wherever our essaying talks have been taking us – and by now, because Gail and I have also established a small publishing venture[2] as a way of increasing our essaying activities, these destinations are proliferating – we find teachers, graduates and undergraduates new to this game must first get over their understanding of a form that is traditionally understood as wanting to marshal and contain thinking, not let it go free.

One of the projects we've been working on, with students at Merton as well as in Scotland, is an exhibition, of sorts, which we've called 'These Windows'. It's an online publication as well as a pamphlet; a series of mini

'Essaying Banners' created by artist Merran Gunn.

essays – fragments in some cases – created in response to the museum collections at the V&A, both in Dundee and in London. We invited students to select, either randomly or by design, an item in one or other of those institutions, and write a piece in response to it. Art students would be on hand, then, to translate the writings – into drawing, prints, designs – and there! A sort of double essaying took place.

Kinetic activity – an energy generated by setting up artists up a conversation between essayists, poets, filmmakers, architecture theorists and more – has been at the heart of our next project , too. 'Imagined Spaces' is a book of essays all based upon the idea of speculative, imaginative collaborations – suggesting one essayist in concert with another, to write together, write alongside, and also write alone... It's that Music Room again, I can hear – and indeed a number of us did join voices around a table there, after a morning of essaying discussions with a group that included Peter Davidson, whose work we'd been reading and who talked of the rich archive of essaying papers – some no more than gestures towards texts – by John Aubrey held in the Bodleian; how they might be brought out into the light as much as any other writing, and allowed to live.

One of the students at Merton had gifted me with a copy of poems by Chantal Miller she had translated. Along with her own essay – about a Persian carpet in the oriental rooms on the ground floor of the V&A in London, 'I... wait for illumination', she writes, half way through her text – a poem by Miller, 'Writing', also seems to speak perfectly of the essaying project entire: 'writing /like deference or like rebellion /without choice /without pause/... like someone who leaves the light on/and sleeps standing over his own body...'.

'These Windows' has been, as suggested by the title, a glimpse onto a view – upon the capabilities and imagination of young people, the kinds of writing they can make when not hounded by the notion of an objective or an argument or a thesis or the stringencies of a 'workshop'. This, along with 'Imagined Spaces', represents a different kind of proposition altogether; there is a 'light on'. Just as I have been thinking about how – as writers of fiction and poetry – the central action of essays remind us of how we get to grips with language, to make it our own, as well as help us learn what's important about what we are trying to do as artists, so, too, might the essays we write be a form of instruction manual, a source book, a sort of personal 'Works and Days'. The American poet Linda Bamber writes an essay about a lone sailor and it becomes a version of a workbook for her own understanding of imagery and praxis and... craft. '*My own universe*, I exulted, as I lost sight of land.' Carl Phillips reaches the end of a long life as a poet and declares, in a recklessly confessional essay, that recklessness in art is all. He quotes a line from 'Damascus'

by Deborah Digges, a poem using the central motif of a massive snapping turtle, stranded on a highway at a 'Cross here or die. Die crossing' the poem finishes; 'Who did I think I was to lift him like a pond,/or ballast from the slosh of hull swamp, tarred as he was, undaunted...'

By really... essaying into the material we provide ourselves with, as writers or as teachers, by exposing ourselves, in essays, to implications we find we've made about other work, by letting ourselves be tainted by writing's risks, so we train ourselves to become fluent in our own writing; we learn its rhythms and feel, its temperature – knowledge that can then be applied to a short story or poem or paragraph in hand. This deepening of our individual eccentric idiolect, this private imaginative language, in due course, comes to be in daily use; our natural way of speaking. As Edwin Muir, sensitive as he was to the dangers of splitting registers, reminds us: 'A language which is used only for poetry is bound to grow poorer, even for poetry purposes, than one which is used for all ends of discourse.' So this essaying of ours helps us look ON in order that we may regard the world from within.

'And as I peered out my mind grew sharper', writes Louise Gluck in 'Nest':

And I remember accurately
the sequence of my responses,
my eyes fixing on each thing
from the shelter of the hidden self:

first, *I love it.*
Then, *I can use it.*

Notes

1 See 'Essaying in the Old Music Room' in *PNR* 254.
2 The Voyage Out Press was established in 2016 to publish essays, poetry and some forms of non-fiction. The first publication of *The Voyage Out* comprised essays, artwork, conversation and fragments; due out in November is 'Imagined Spaces', a further volume of collaborative and solo essays. The Voyage Out Press also published *These Windows* earlier this year. Details can be found at https://dura-dundee.org.uk/category/essay/; and https://dura-dundee.org.uk.

Carl Phillips, 'Foliage', in *The Kenyon Review*, Fall 2014, Vol XXXVI, Number 4.

Linda Bamber's poetry collection *Metropolitan Tang* and her short stories *Taking What I Like* are published by Black Sparrow Press.

Chantal Miller, *Killing Plato*, trans. By Yvette Siegert, New Directions.

Two Poems

MAUREEN N. McLANE

Correspondent Breeze

for Tom Pickard

I.

two hawks above Park Avenue –
      on what draft –
April's chilling us back into March

season's out of joint Tom

*

Lincoln Tunnel
Holland Tunnel
wind tunnel

*

no fuckwinds here
but fuck, the wind's
my ears' bane, then
a caress

*

what should have come
to you last spring –
that wind, these lines

II.

reservoir surface blown
north, a new year, January
wind and the white underbellies
of geese here for the season

*

O Canada see how they come
despite a border
wind knows no wall
it can't blow by or through

*

the prevailing winds
prevail, the westerlies wester
& that gust gusted
up a schoolgirl's skirt,
the bare tree's branch

*

Fiends Fell walked
in the mind, that clough
where they sought shelter
a shelter in the mind –

border trouble
border slumber
a Westron wind blowing
to you, friend

False Spring

False spring: then a blanketing
of ice recalling you to your senses
and the true season.

The trees taken
unaware, stunned in their
clear ice sheaths.

For each limb
and nub its own
ice coat.

No reason
for surprise, yet walking
in the park it stopped

you dead to hear
the casings crack
in the wind.

No helpless melting.
No slow drip.
Each trunk and branch within

a cold casket.
No one to kiss,
no promise of release.

A History of Sunburn

ROBERT MINHINNICK

UV levels increase in the spring across the UK,
reaching a peak in late June.

In this current spell of fine weather, we could see
some of the highest UV levels ever recorded.

'Normally they're about six or seven in the summer
months', says BBC Weather's Matt Taylor. 'Today we
could hit a nine in some parts of southern England
and South Wales.'

                                        BBC News, June 25, 2020

On June 12, 1945,
Albert Minhinnick had written in his diary:
                        This is one of the worst
                        malaria areas in the world.
                        Also cholera. What a dump....

...while 75 years later
I'm walking the lanes to Picton Court
to verify how you are, recalling
that you said Albert always kept a mouthful
in his canteen, while the other soldiers
finished every drop...

              First thing
I note is three of your friends
out on the grass in straw hats,
the nurses wearing orange masks.
Not long ago, I could have told
what villages those nurses come from.

But you're in bed
and I'm talking through the double glazing
and you're not hearing.
We're all thinking of you, I say finally.
Shouting love. Miming love. Turning away.

Perhaps you hear me but I go back,
past the horses we're told not to touch,
and avoiding a woman coming in the opposite
   direction
in her own mask.

Ah, sweet embraceable you! I want to say.
Am I the monster from your imagination,
unmasked and anonymous, looming
out of the honeysuckle?
Behind me stands Cefn Bryn on Gower.
I've always thought it my personal volcano,
its long eruption burying us
in invisible ash.

They've cut the wheat, its stubble
almost white, and sharp as limestone.
My watch has stopped
but this could be any hour
in the last ten thousand years, and my mother
is looking at the screen because Matt Taylor
is speaking again, all about UV.

So I think of Albert in his own June,
watching the cobra moving past the cookhouse,
writing how ten weeks after VE Day
                        the Japs attacked last night.
and one week later *the Welch*
suffered very heavy casualties ...

And on August 8, *Atomic bomb is used on Japan...*
a ghastly weapon this
but should end the war quickly...

Then on Wednesday, August 14, he writes
                        peace in the world
but one of the horses is wearing a fly-sheet
to save it from sunburn, and soon
my lips are crusted and my tongue
flickering in the air like that snake.

Yet I keep thinking of Albert, twenty,
with mules and wireless, guarding his water ration,
and writing a diary for people
he never thought about. And I suppose
that's exactly what history is,
        like my last sight of you, behind the glass,
        raising your hand and mouthing words
        impossible to hear...

Something Momentous Like a War
Text and Pandemic
RACHEL HADAS

Intertextuality, according to Wikipedia, is 'the shaping of a text's meaning by another text. It is the interconnection between similar or related works of literature that reflect or influence an audience's interpretation of the text....'.

I often tell my students that intertextuality is a cumbersome and abstract word (Bernard O'Donoghue, in his *Poetry: A Very Short Introduction,* politely calls the term 'rather elaborate') for a very simple principle: that texts refer to other texts, because that's the nature of texts – and it's our human nature too, to connect. Admittedly, the term has its utility; it refers to something real. Nouns, however clumsy, have a function when what they're naming exists.

But I can't think of a good name for another principle related to reading that also certainly exists – the way texts can suddenly, urgently refer to our lives at the moment we're reading them. Relatable, my students sometimes say. Reader-response, like intertextuality is an off-puttingly-theoretical term for a process that comes so naturally it seems intuitive; and the same might be said of receptionsaesthetik. Thich Nat Hanh's term 'interbeing' comes a bit closer to what I have in mind, as does, if I understand it, the notion of cosmic interdependence to which the term 'Indra's Net' refers. Neither interbeing nor Indra's Net refers particularly to reading, but both terms signify a vision that embraces everything, so that any tiny thing – a leaf, a bug, a tear, a breath of wind, or a paragraph – can encompass and call up immensity. Nothing's irrelevant, nothing should be dismissed; everything somehow fits, and everything merits our attention – and more than merits it, commands it.

Thus I could be thinking about any phenomenon at all – but here I'm thinking about reading. Maybe the term I want is connectivity – not my favorite, but it may have to do.

When we connect something we're reading to our lives, the author's conscious intention in writing a passage may have nothing to do with the use to which we put that passage – that is, the meaning or pleasure we derive from it, the life-shaped slot into which we can't help tucking it. In the case of a passage from Homer or Shakespeare, for example, chronology clearly rules out the author's intentionally inserting the precise meaning that the reader then extracts, since that reader was unborn when the text was written. And yet to say that the writer's intention has nothing to do with the reader's interpretation isn't the whole story. For that 'nothing to do with' overlooks the salient fact of the shared humanity of writer and reader across time and space. Whitman captures this gap, and bridges it, in 'Crossing Brooklyn Ferry', where he addresses readers of the future in terms of the human experience that connects him to them: 'time avails not, distance avails not.'

Whatever the writer's intention, which is often unrecoverable or unknown even while that writer is still alive, readers cannot help making these connections, these leaps across time and space. And this connectivity is especially likely to happen, we're especially likely to pounce upon a nugget of meaning, if we're experiencing a difficult patch in our own lives. When you're bereaved, you see grief and loss everywhere. A Rutgers colleague of mine, a Renaissance scholar who had often taught Macchiavelli's *The Prince,* found that he read it differently after the sudden death of his wife. Now he was looking for clues about Machiavelli's attitude to emotion – even though, as he dryly puts it, 'The *Prince* has yet to be assigned reading for anybody experiencing grief'.

Another unexpected example of connectivity came in a letter I recently received about a poem of mine, 'Love and Dread'. The poem is about lots of themes – joy and terror, the beginning and the end of life. The writer of this very kind letter had been making a practice of thanking poets, among them me, for 'words that have added meaning to my experience'. She went on to assure me that 'I don't presume that in this poem you're literally discussing sobriety, but as I read it I can't help thinking about how I felt after my first few recovery meetings...'. Certainly an unexpected connection. But if my phrases in the poem 'the clamor of chaos everywhere' and 'life bestows gifts past expectation' meant something specific to this young woman in the light of her own powerful experience, so much the better. Meaning in poetry – in literature – has the same generative and self-renewing quality as names do, or anything that one can keep and pass on at the same time.

Examples of this kind of connectivity could be multiplied (why, for example, do lovers like to read love poems?). But I want to move to connectivity in the context of the overwhelming experience we've all been sharing to one degree or another for – is it only three months? The principle is the same: we can't help connecting a great deal of what we're reading or rereading to what's going on in and beyond our lives, especially when what's going on is so powerful.

Since the middle of March, I know I have not been alone in experiencing a feeling that one of my students captured eloquently in her final exam in April: 'events that seem... unrealistic and imaginary can actually happen'. On the one hand, fiction suddenly seems more plausible; but by the same token, life feels closer to fiction – and to poetry. These days we read both fiction and poetry differently; and we connect them more closely with our own experience. And this difference, this new alertness to connections, applies not only when we're reading the Iliad or Thucydides or Boccaccio or Defoe or Camus. Of course the larger situation of a plague descending on a city or country or the whole world is something we're now hypervigilant for, hypersensitive to. But much smaller details also become something to pause over. Or, rather, they reach out and grab us as we read.

I became acquainted with this sensation some fifteen years ago, when I was first attempting to digest the massive and unpalatable reality of my then husband's dementia. His insidious illness had been diagnosed only after years of willful blindness (my denial, his denial, everyone's denial). Cavafy's poem 'Walls' took on a dire new meaning.

With no consideration, no pity, no shame,
they have built walls around me, thick and high.
And now I sit here feeling hopeless.
I can't think of anything else: this fate gnaws
     my mind –
because I had so much to do outside.
When they were building the walls, how could I not
     have noticed!
But I never heard the builders, not a sound.
Imperceptibly they have closed me off from the
     outside world.
        (Translated by Edmund Keeley)

And in answer to the inevitable questions trouble and illness provoke – Why this suffering? Who's to blame? Why now? – Hardy's 'The Subalterns', a poem I stumbled on at this same period of my life, gave me these indelible stanzas:

'To-morrow I attack thee, wight',
     Said Sickness. 'Yet I swear
I bear thy little ark no spite,
     But am bid enter there.'

'Come hither, Son', I heard Death say;
     'I did not will a grave
Should end thy pilgrimage to-day,
     But I, too, am a slave!'

We smiled upon each other then,
     And life to me had less
Of that fell look it wore ere when
     They owned their passiveness.

Those poems read one way to me in 2005 and 2006; then they went out of focus for a while. Now they're back, with a vengeance. Cavafy's insidious walls convey the claustrophobic feeling of lockdown – 'they have closed me off from the outside world'. More than that, the sly inconspicuousness with which the walls were built (and just who are 'the builders'?) recalls the stealthy progress of the virus, moving around the globe while we all 'had so much to do outside'. Similarly, Hardy's personified yet bureaucratically impersonal Sickness, which has nothing against us but is 'bid' to 'enter' us, could well be COVID-19.

Part of what I'm describing here is the way texts renew themselves for us again and again, depending on the situation. Some examples are spiced with incongruity. Currently, rereading Henry James's novella *The Spoils of Poynton,* I've been struck by a sentence that I hadn't remembered, or had never noticed, on a first reading many years before: 'She couldn't leave her own house without peril of exposure.' James uses infection as a metaphor; but what happens to a metaphor when we're living in a world where we literally can't leave our houses without peril of exposure?

Ever since Susan Sontag's *Illness as Metaphor,* we've often been cautioned not to liken the experience of illness to fighting a battle. But what if, as many people including my dental hygienist neighbor have pointed out, the process of donning PPE does indeed resemble arming for battle with a fearsome enemy? And we've all gotten used to talking about people serving on the front lines. War and pandemic, pandemic and war; it's hard to read (or talk) about one without thinking of the other. In Anthony Powell's novel *Temporary Kings,* set in the 1950s, the narrator muses about what it is that attracts people to reunions with old companions from the war. But as the phrasing at the outset makes clear, the reunion phenomenon ('How was your war?') extends beyond shared military experience:

When something momentous like a war has taken place, all existence turned upside down, personal life discarded, every relationship reorganized, there is a temptation, after all is over, to return to what remains of the machine, examine such paraphernalia as came one's way, pick about among the bent and rusting composite parts, assess merits and defects.

Rereading this passage recently, I immediately connected 'something momentous' to the pandemic. Not that everyone's personal life has been discarded; but 'all existence turned upside down' seems pretty applicable, as does that temptation many of us, and not only editorialists, politicians, and academic administrators, are already feeling to look back, 'after all is over' (which isn't yet), 'to return to what remains of the machine'. We'll be looking at institutions and at society; we'll be asking each other 'How was your quarantine?'; 'What was the pandemic like for you?'.

Even before 'all is over', our momentous experience right now (Powell's adjective fits our current situation perfectly) makes us look at texts differently – and also look back differently at texts we thought we knew. Given passages can come to seem uncannily proleptic. In March, when the ugly and inaccurate term 'social distancing' swiftly became part of our daily vocabulary and directed our daily behavior, I was reminded of the celebrated passage in the *Odyssey* where Odysseus, visiting the underworld, encounters the shade of his mother. He wants to hug her:

How I longed
To embrace my mother's spirit, dead as she was!
Three times I rushed toward her, desperate to hold
     her,
Three times she fluttered through my fingers, sifting
     away
Like a shadow, dissolving like a dream, and each time
The grief cut to the heart, sharper, yes, and I,

I cried out to her, words winging into the darkness:
'Mother – why not wait for me? – How I long to hold
    you! –
so even here, in the house of Death, we can fling
our loving arms around each other, take some joy
in the tears that numb the heart.'
      (*Odyssey* XI 233–45, tr. Robert Fagles)

This passage, imitated by Virgil when Aeneas, visiting the underworld, encounters the shade of his father, no longer seemed 'unrealistic and imaginary', in my student's words. On the contrary, it described and still describes an experience that more and more people came to feel viscerally when it was a question of loved ones far away, or even not so far away but as physically inaccessible as the dead. The trouble with Zoom is that it doesn't allow hugs. Only today, an article in the *New York Times* suggested some relatively safe hugging modalities, because we human beings so manifestly need to hug and to be hugged.

This visceral ache, this tug of war between emotional and physical need and distance, is the subject of Shakespeare's sonnets 46 and particularly 47. I quote only the latter, though both should be read together; the astonishing line in 46, which refers to the heart as 'A closet never pierc'd with crystal eyes', is worth a lot of thought in our glassy era:

Betwixt mine eye and heart a league is took,
And each doth good turns now unto the other.
When that mine eye is famish'd for a look
Or heart in love with sighs himself doth smother,
With my love's picture then my eye doth feast,
And to the painted banquet bids my heart.
Another time mine eye is my heart's guest,
And in his thoughts of love doth share a part.
So either by thy picture or my love,
Thyself away are present still with me;
For thou no farther than my thoughts canst move,
And I am still with them, and thee with thee;
Or if they sleep, thy picture in my sight
Awakes my heart to heart's and eye's delight.

If for 'heart' we substitute something like 'emotional need' or 'longing' or even 'the desire to reach out and touch', this poem perfectly captures the frustrating dilemma of feeling 'famished for a look' – and yet how satisfying can a 'painted banquet', 'love's picture', a mere visual, be?

That same sense of the hungry gaze, which seems so wrenchingly relevant to our current state of separation, is the subject of a wonderful paragraph in a student's recent answer to a question on a take-home exam about how the pandemic had affected her sense of what she was reading. In discussing Margaret Atwood's *The Penelopiad,* Chelsea is of course referring to a text which has an intertextual relationship to the *Odyssey.* But she goes one step further, away from Homer and straight into Atwood and thence to 2020:

In examining the quarantine aspect of this pandemic, I felt a resemblance to deceased Penelope in Margaret

Atwood's *The Penelopiad.* Every day we are forced to stay within the confines of our own homes; restricted from the outside world and only connected by what seems to be a window looking out. In this way, I feel the same way Penelope did when she peered out from the underworld: 'Every once in a while the fogs part and we get a glimpse of the world of the living. It's like rubbing the glass on a dirty window, making space to look through.' (Atwood 17) Like Penelope, we are trapped behind the fog of anxiety and the unseen attacks of the virus itself. All we can do is remain trapped inside our own homes and hope the fog parts every so often to see the light the world has to offer.

By referring to a passage in Atwood's novel which (departing from Atwood's intertextual dependence on Homer) turns out to have a subtle and poignant relevance to our present moment, Chelsea elegantly illustrates an unexpected and powerful connection between a text and life as lived right now.

In her 1926 essay 'On Being Ill', Virginia Woolf ponders: 'one would have thought that novels... would have been devoted to influenza; epic poems to typhoid; odes to pneumonia; lyrics to toothache.' A passage in this essay anticipates the image in *The Penelopiad* which reminded my student Chelsea of the deprivations of quarantine. Woolf compares the sick person to someone gazing disconsolately through a smudged pane of glass – except that instead of a window, the glass appears to be the body which encases the besieged soul: 'The creature within can only gaze through the pane – smudged or rosy ; it cannot separate off from the body like the sheath of a knife or the pod of a pea for a single instant.'

Woolf is here describing the experience of illness from within; Penelope in *The Penelopiad* is telling us how the dead can occasionally catch glimpses of the living; and Chelsea is evoking the sensation of a healthy person who is cooped up. From their respective angles, all three passages approach one experience: the sensation of being isolated, even imprisoned – a way of living which in our current pandemic is one of the ways we can try to protect ourselves.

That sense of isolation as protection came up for me recently with wry urgency in an unexpected place – but then many overlaps between text and life do seem to emerge in unexpected places. Putting in a vegetable garden earlier this spring, we were reminded that a large woodchuck, familiar to us from past years (unless it was some woodchuck forbear we remembered), was living under an old apple tree at the far end of the vegetable patch. Once we started looking and asking, lore about woodchucks turned out, of course, to be abundant – how many doors their burrows have; how hard they are to get rid of; various repellants one might try. Then I remembered that Robert Frost has a poem about woodchucks.

'A Drumlin Woodchuck' begins in the first person but soon switches to third. By the fourth of this poem's eight quatrains, the woodchuck is speaking not only for all woodchucks but also very possibly for all creatures who are intent on surviving. In a time of holing up or hunkering down or sheltering in place – choose your phrase – the woodchuck's way of coping has a lesson for everyone. Here are the poem's final three stanzas:

> And if after the hunt goes past
> And the double-barreled blast
> (Like war and pestilence
> And the loss of common sense),
>
> I can with confidence say
> That still for another day,
> Or even another year,
> I will be there for you, my dear,
>
> It will be because, though small
> As measured against the All,
> I have been so instinctively thorough
> About my crevice and burrow.

It was easy to see the relevance of the final two lines. But only on a fifth or sixth reading did I finally notice the word 'pestilence'. Born in 1874, Frost lived through both the First World War and the 1918 pandemic. It seems entirely possible that the hunt thundering past 'with double-barreled blast' while the woodchuck prudently stays underground is the Four Horsemen of the Apocalypse, or at least two of those four horsemen.

Because I wasn't expecting 'A Drumlin Woodchuck' to be about a pandemic, I was struck first by the poem's preoccupation with shelter and survival, whether on the animal or the human levels. But pestilence is there too, and war and pestilence are more threatening to people than they are to woodchucks. (Katherine Anne Porter's 1939 novella *Pale Horse, Pale Rider* is about, precisely, those two of the four apocalyptic horsemen.) By 1936, when 'A Drumlin Woodchuck' was collected in his volume *A Further Range,* Frost had survived both war and pestilence; 'instinctively thorough' about sheltering, he was still there. The place where my husband and I have been holing up, or hunkering down, happens to be in rural Vermont. A local friend recently reminded me that 'woodchuck' is an affectionate (or more or less affectionate?) term for a Vermonter.

It's one thing, as one reads, to come upon texts from Homer to Frost that seem to pertain to our present crisis. To find such proleptic passages in one's own recent work is something else again. Or is it? I observed earlier that an author's intention is hard to discern even during their lifetime. More than that , the author may well be uncertain of her own intention in writing what she wrote. Maybe there was no conscious, specific intention – which is one reason poets, and maybe other writers too, dislike being asked 'What were you trying to say?'.

So I'd like to close by pivoting from my reading of other people's writing, and seeing how that writing connects to our COVID moment, to considering a few of the poems I wrote before March 2020. My intention in these earlier poems, whatever that intention was, isn't the point; their uncanny relevance is.

My poems draw a lot – not exclusively, but a lot – from dream imagery. Dreams and some poems share a charged, ambiguous space between past and future. Like the Mirror of Galadriel in Tolkien's *The Lord of the Rings,* both can seem to show a vivid picture of something, an image that captures some essential truth. But whether that picture belongs to the past, present, or future isn't easy to tell. The prophet Calchas is described early in the Iliad as one who knows what is, what will be, and what was; dreams can seem to work that way too.

Of the poems I wrote in 2018 and 2019 that I've been returning to, those that seem to fit into what is now a present and what was then a future reflect two preoccupations; contain two sets of images. Naturally, both these preoccupations originally connected to realities other than the pandemic, but as they read now both are all too easily applicable to the pandemic.

In April 2019, I fell and hurt my leg. Waiting in an ER cubicle to be X-rayed, I turned on the tiny television angled above my bed – and there was Notre Dame in flames. Was the tiny glassy image even real? In a poem entitled 'Same Screen', which owes nothing to dreams but plenty to reality recalled, I recall a couple of experiences of glassy remoteness, beginning with the food at Horn and Hardart's Automat, when I used to be taken there as a child, displayed behind thick glass windows and ending with Hart Crane's line from 'To Brooklyn Bridge': 'Foretold to other eyes on the same screen.' My poem also remembers the line from Ionesco's absurdist play *The Bald Soprano:* 'a stone caught fire.' How could a stone burn? And yet there was Notre Dame before my eyes, on fire – or rather, an image of Notre Dame on a small screen. 'Same Screen', which was written in April and May 2019, had a refrain: 'Behind glass, behind glass.' I couldn't know at the time that behind glass, the same screen, would come in less than a year to be where much of life was conducted.

Several poems I wrote in 2018 and 2019 are grappling both with my experiences in the classroom and with my knowledge that in not very many more years, I'd be retiring. How did that knowledge feel? The poems give a clear picture of cloudy feelings, and they all do draw on dream imagery. 'Teaching the Tigers' accurately depicts a dream-derived image of a large and somewhat unruly class I was teaching at the time, all facing me, all masked. The poem reads in part:

> Arms folded, wearing tiger masks,
> students sit. Questions? No one asks.
>
> Loss and grief, exile, return:
> How much of it can they take in?
>
> The Iliad: to go to war.
> The Odyssey: and come back home.
>
> Epic's relentless forward motion,
> lyric's gossamer attention,
>
> adventure parsed as allegory,
> the iterations of the story,
>
> and then to choose the right translation
> for a fearful generation.
>
> May poetry keep finding ways
> of piercing the miasmal haze
>
> and reclaiming a clear space
> behind each young and guarded face

and washing through the walls that hide
whatever's bubbling inside.

The masks, the miasma, the walls that need to be pierced, the fear, the guardedness – they're all here. Coincidence? Very possibly.

In 'Tiger Stripes', the tiger masks of the previous poem seem to melt and morph into one tiger, languorous and lazy, prowling the streets of a deserted city, where the one named building is the Anxiety Hotel. I know a dream contributed to this poem too, but I don't recall it as well as I do the tiger mask dream. Did the images of the empty city come from this second dream? I don't remember. But read now, the poem is about disruption, melting down. The concluding stanzas read:

Camouflage stripes of gold and brown:
the tiger world is melting down.
Caught in a beam of morning sun,
massive transitions are going on,
each nation and each generation
vying for who will take possession
of the Hotel Anxiety.
(Who wants to manage it? Not me).
Who gets to stay? Who has to go?
Process laborious and slow.
Who moves ahead? Who stays behind?
Musclebound combatants grunt and grind.
Who's the owner? Who's the heir?
And will the fearful future care?

Striped camouflage of grey and black:
there's never any turning back.
Once the place is emptied out,
what was all the fuss about?
The fissures in the family,
the rivalry, the enmity:
door now ajar, each vacant suite,
blank windows staring at the street,
hotel abandoned, no life left –
we barely even feel bereft.

Camouflage stripes of grey and brown,
the tiger world is winding down.
Disruption on a local scale –
no one is forwarding the mail.
Shadows slide down a blank wall.
Our hotel is very small.
The stripes are vibrating: illusion,
the camouflage of our confusion.
The cat sits up and licks his paws.
We're all obedient to laws
too big to assimilate.
It's still early. And it's late.

The fearful future (that word 'fearful' again); the world melting or winding down; the vacant suite with its blank windows; disruption; the small hotel; the laws too big to assimilate. What did I have in mind when I wrote this poem? I'm not sure. It's tempting, though, however impossible it would be to prove, to say the coming 'invisible' pandemic, after an 'interlude out of sight / curled up away from noise and light', had me in mind, was writing through me. We're told that viruses have no character, no consciousness, no purpose except to replicate. But my own fearful subconscious seemed to be aware of a not-human force inexorably approaching.

Another dream-based poem I wrote in 2019 also features emptied-out spaces. A leopard pads down the aisle of a classroom; the tiger-masked students reappear (in bringing them back, I was most likely referring not to a dream but to my earlier poem). Is 'The Last Lecture Hall' such a valedictory poem because I was mulling over endings? From the vantage point of June 2020, as I write this and as college administrators struggle with impossible decisions about reopening their institutions in the fall, the lastness isn't the farewell of a departing professor but an elegiac vision of a space that is itself on the way out, or that will be transformed. 'The Last Lecture Hall' reads in part:

Theaters that were never ours,
classrooms empty and refill.

We cross the stage and disappear...
The empty theater becomes

a lecture hall...
Tiger-masked students fill the seats

of the amphitheater...

Lights go on in the theater.
We stumble out. Class is over.

As schools and colleges struggle to achieve social distancing, lecture halls may well be replaced by amphitheaters.

In early February 2020, a dream that didn't make it into a poem presented me with the image of a hospital bed somewhere deep within the marble bowels of Columbia's Low Library. Less than two months later, some colleges were being asked to fill their dorm rooms with hospital beds.

It might be said that the images in my dreams, like the images in all dreams, are archetypal, nonspecific; this may well be. Certainly the dreams, like all dreams, are capable of multiple interpretations. Like most dreams, these present a series of vivid images rather than story lines. Nevertheless, the proleptic aptness of some of the images these dreams fished up remains remarkable.

All these dreams of mine, dreams I only remember because I spun poems out of them, seem so vividly congruent with the waking world as it manifested after the poems were written. Likewise, all the texts I've been considering here could easily translate into the realm of dreams. In this period of pandemic, our lives feel bafflingly double: nightmarish and yet quotidian, outlandish yet bound by routine, unimaginable and yet pressingly real, severely limited in space but curiously fluid as to time. Stuck in the 'very small' Anxiety Hotel, we can still read, and dream, and remember. Bounded in a nutshell, we can, for moments at least, count ourselves a king of infinite space. Unable to see our friends except on a glassy screen, we can feel companioned by the throngs of predecessors who somehow saw this moment approaching (didn't they?), and who wrote about it.

Three Poems

PAUL STEPHENSON

Day Hectic

I'd just doored the get-in when the red ring phoned.
Living into the running room, I received the pick-up,
eared it wearily to my hold. An enquired voice: *Hello?*
I'm froming the call... can I glaze you in double-interested?

I colden hate-callers: *No!* Mouthpiecing down the slam,
I blazered my hang-up, shoed off too-tight kicks, sighed,
saw evening windows streaming August through the light.
The peace seemed strangely at room, but then I noticed...

mantel the besidepiece a walling had painted off the fall,
must have bookcased behind the slide. To reach it meant
hardbacking all the take-outs, stacking them in carefuls
of spine-worn crime – tedious and it would take a time.

I gently landscaped the salvage – a favourite take-me-to
my used-to mother beached – grandfathered by my oil-do
the die before he yeared. Two-inching in a deep hammer,
I levelled back a bit to check it was stand. Less or more.

Seven gone. I stomached my hearing, rumbled a faint feel.
Kitchening to the walk I worsened the expect and fridging
the open, milked nothing except spot. A choice basically
between omeletting a knock-up or egging a couple of boils.

Radioing the switch-on, the old same. They were invading
the far discussion somewhere latest, moraling its questions.
I placed a lay for myself, stale-soldiered my bread into cuts,
birded to the listens, yolking their heads deep into the dunk.

An adult I refuse to believe

in voting for either of the two main
course followed by dessert or cheese
can lead to the build-up of fatty
boom boom sweet sugar dumpling
recipe for that perfectly stodgy stew
in his own juice as far as I'm
watching the trailer for the latest

on the ship set sail to take Syria's
leading natural resource and chief
police officers providing expertise in
Shadow Priest updated to Patch 8.2
release date pushed back two weeks
'Until the End of Time' by Justin
posted a photo of him cuddling up

to no good as you might expect
decent returns on your investment
cycles and a variety of market
this little piggy stayed at home
appliances from the UK's largest
breeds including the English
flag is composed of a large red

wine you can lay down and keep
away from talk of religion or race
to be the first nation to set foot
and mouth disease spreading fast
profits reading fair and square
up with you later if you don't mind
games to improve IQ and stave off

work owing to stress and anxiety
costing the country an estimated
fetal length and weight based on
the open-source android operating
hours extended over the festive
activities in Shakespeare Country
properties to buy as a second home

Office issued a statement denying
her rights of access to the three
Graces carved in white marble
cake with swirls of light sponge
off the NHS for free medical
gloves made of latex to prevent
a backlash against the new proposal.

Trieste
(*tredici modi di guardare una città*)

1. Trace the cars with your feet
    cutting the city apart.

2. Traffic takes the Habsburgs hostage.
    Ransom on the sea.

3. Streets traipse uphill
    past a museum of laminates.

4. Trees foreground the process
    of conjuring Ulysses.

5. In this triangular stream
    of consciousness, read on.

6. Is unification
    trespassing on tomorrow?

    (In Piazza Unità d'Italia
    tromboni).

7. Rejoice! On its way! See the tray
    of iced Camparis.

8. TripAdvisor says choose
    from one hundred thousand rooms.

9. Enough of words. Tired tongues
    make a truce: gelato.

10. Try stracciatella
    or ricotta stregata?

11. Couples trail the waterfront:
    black midnight territory.

    (In the head's narrow strip
    new troops stand at the crossroads).

12. A tryst, assignation,
    a tried assassination.

13. Katabatic winds,
    trapped in the meaning of nowhere.

Elaine

KATRIONA FEINSTEIN

for my grandmother

It's six months after
you accepted the anticipated silence.
Wettest February on record,
and something in the meanders
of my evening bus ride recalls
those exhausted journeys home.
Suddenly, physically, I miss you.

I fire up my phone. Time to listen
for counsel from ghosts, my hospice recordings.
It takes just a bleating alarm
to seize me. I'm sucked back
to all those hours at your bedside,
picking at berries, swapping kisses.
I long for that singular purpose,
shepherding those pressured cells
to connect with easy warmth
on family matters, poet friends
and the relent of summer
in your foreign room made home
by daily troops of devotees.

And it's with surprise I find,
as much as I try to feel sad, I can't.
Elaine, you'll have to excuse the clichés this time:
it seems I only think of you and smile.

Lolling together on your sofa
after the customary peppered steak and buttered
    beans.
Watching among rows of strangers
or across from you at Thursday lunch,
with a child's pride I never lost,
as you took fierce command of every word
and wrung from each a brazen truth as best you knew:
our tribal elder, svelte in glitter.
And we listened.
An earlier you cried out last summer,
so I curled up in your bed
and we lay in nestled silence.
I relished the tightness of your
loose-skinned grip, your gosling hair.
You trudged forwards,
tender and steadfast as ever,
in your battle for the dawn.

One thing you should know:
I finally started to write.
Poetry, no less.
A little later than you hoped –
just a week after your death –
but I think you'd cheer this triumph
then quickly press me to forge ahead,
in case I lose the courage,
nursed in no small part by your
gentle words at last starting to take root.
'She's a bit shy!' you informed
my dad with impatience,
but you saw iron lurking behind
a timeworn petticoat of grins.
'You see, I can't help knowing things,'
you told me once, and it was true.
Thanks to you, I've learned to let
the less dignified emotions sing.

So on this swampy miserable night,
buffeted by a London bus on diversion,
I stop and laugh, summoning
your misplaced proofs, chaotic Passovers,
mysterious cupboard jars
decades out of date.
And that vast varnished wooden desk,
knighted with green leather,
always besieged by bills,
bolting letters, printed emails.
A noble setting for your daily tussles
with the Apple Mac.

All at once past tense –
this is not yet within my reach –
and it's left to us to go on ageing.
But these life-threads are treasures
and remain for us a celebration.

Genesis and Other Poems
WILLIAM LOGAN

Genesis

I.
In the Beginning was the Worm.

II.
In the Beginning was the Verb.

Spring Among the Fallen

The weather took hold, pollen
skimming the windows
with a handful of saffron.

The neighbor's ornamental
burst into miniature fireworks,
its once-a-year holiday.

Not all endings were recalled.
The temporary music
was heard in absence, racket

and squall of the dawn chorus,
the chill of late-departed winter
a loss disguised as piety.

Through the planted beds, rumors
abounded, the resurrection ferns
in their selfish unwindings,

the slow crawl of the judicial snail,
bees begging at the windows,
then the slate curtain of rain.

We were late and out of time.

That, Dying

That, dying, you were not dead,
propped on the shadows of an unmade bed,
paper at your side, unread,
that, dying you were not dead.

That, dying, you were not dead,
there were things left to do. Instead,
you ate a buttered piece of bread,
that, dying, you were not dead.

That, dying, you were not dead,
you knew that nothing lay ahead,
nothing past the lingering dread
that, dying, you were not dead.

That, dying, you were not dead,
the room was left uninhabited,
yet still you left so much unsaid,
the ground below the darkness overhead,

that, dying, you were not dead.

With Lowry in Cuernavaca

RICHARD GWYN

Caminar en esta zona no le recomiendo: es muy peligroso, said the security guard on the graveyard shift at my hotel in Cuernavaca, as I set out for a midnight stroll. 'I don't recommend walking in this area: it's very dangerous.' I am staying at the Hacienda Cortés, a sugar mill built in 1530 by the conquistador, Hernán Cortés, for the son he had with his mistress, La Malinche, and worked by the family – or rather, their slaves – until it fell into disuse and was, much later, reinvented as a hotel. Guests are housed in small bungalows, each with its own tiny patio garden.

Earlier there was a storm, rocking the trees outside my room, which shed leaves like thin leathery hands and a quantity of other solid matter, along with a downpour of such intensity that I put off heading downtown, settling instead for the more local comforts of the hotel restaurant.

On the latest leg of my Mexican journey, I have just spent a day and a night in Mexico City, returning to the capital from Veracruz to attend a *tertulia,* a literary discussion group organised by the poet Fabio Morábito and friends. Afterwards I visited the barrio of Mixcoac, passing Octavio Paz's family home en route, before returning to the more familiar territory of Condesa, and dinner at Luigi's with Pedro Serrano and Carlos López Beltrán.

The night before, I broke the journey from Veracruz by stopping off at the town of Puebla, where I had made vague plans to meet up with yet another poet. There, I witnessed an incident, insignificant in itself, which I could not shake off. As I was walking into town, an Indian woman – 'Indian' is not considered to be an offensive term in Mexico and Central America – utterly bedraggled, with long grey hair and dressed in rags, came running past me, chasing after a huge SUV, crying out, at volume and with some distress 'Don Roberto, Don Roberto...'. She carried on at pace up the street calling out *Don Robé... Don Robé...* for an entire block, and I followed her until I could see the vehicle turning at the next set of lights. When I got to the junction, she had stopped, and was resting, hands on knees, her crevassed face fallen into a state of resigned torment. She seemed elderly, although poverty and stress and struggle probably added twenty years to her features. I asked her if she needed help, but she seemed not to see me. I asked again: 'Are you all right?' And she stared at me as if I were mad, as though the question – *estás bien?* – were so idiotic as to defy rational consideration. I cannot imagine what her story was, or what she felt she was owed by the object of her chase, the cruel, oblivious Don Roberto. Quite possibly, of course, she was delusional, and there was no 'Don Roberto' in the car that had driven away, only a random stranger, but the quality of her distress convinced me that some terrible injustice had been committed against her. The scenario was timeless, and her gasping of the honorific 'Don', as her spindly legs carried her in desperate pursuit somehow epitomized the gulf between want and privilege; his status and her subjugation. The image stayed with me as I rode the bus to Mexico City the following day, the massive form of Popocatépetl to my left caught fuzzily on my phone camera above the misty woodlands and broad meadows that gather around its base. The journey impressed on me the extraordinary diversity of the landscape; that within a few hours one can pass from the coast, across prairie, forest and the high sierra. The only constant is the truly terrible music being played full volume wherever you go.

Back on the bus to Cuernavaca, the perennial Mexican bus, we pass through the sprawling shanty outskirts of southern Mexico City and into the mist again. Daily travel awakens in the traveler a sense of permanent dislocation, which is of course what the word means; displacement, an absence of *locus*. I am drawn to Cuernavaca, not only for its alleged splendour, lying as it does, under the volcano – 'plumed with emerald snow and drenched with brilliance' – and the setting for Malcolm Lowry's magnificent, terrible novel of that name, but also because my friend, Peter, who died destitute on the streets of Athens thirty years ago, came here sometime in the 1970s in search of Lowry's ghost, and to drink mescal.

I plan to read *Under the Volcano* in its proper setting, and I take my copy along with me to the dining room. Within an hour or so I am just as astonished – more so perhaps, because better able to acknowledge the scope of the achievement – by Lowry's novel as I was the first time I read it, half a lifetime ago. I digest Michael Schmidt's 'Introduction' along with the chicken consommé, intrigued to discover that Schmidt grew up in the same streets that backdrop the story; and so I proceed to consume the first few chapters with my steak, *nopales* and avocado, washed down with a bottle of Chilean red, and I linger over dessert (fig tartlet and pistachio ice cream), then order coffee and a tequila. I have not eaten so much in months, and certainly not since my arrival in Mexico. By eleven, I have been reading for over three hours, having forgotten enough of the story for it to read like new.

In Lowry's novel, we accompany the ex-Consul, Geoffrey Firmin, as he lives out the last day of his life – which also happens to be the Day of the Dead, November 2nd, 1938 – in Cuernavaca, which Lowry calls by its Nahuatl name, Quauhnahuac. Much of the novel is recounted in a stream of consciousness, describing the lurid visions of a man in the throes of alcoholic meltdown. The novel also narrates the events of the day in the external or material world, in which Geoffrey's estranged wife, Yvonne, returns to him after a separation of several months. Others present – for at least a part of the Consul's final day – are his half-brother Hugh, who has been intimately involved with Yvonne in the past, and is still attracted to her, the film director Laruelle (another of Yvonne's ex-lovers), and a cast of minor characters who inhabit the actual town, as well as the infernal multitudes that populate Geoffrey Firmin's increasingly haunted imagination as the story unfolds with steadily measured suspense – but with all the digressions of a mind in the throes of disintegration – towards its hallucinatory and terrifying climax. This duality, between the inner and the outer, between the spectacular writhing of Firmin's tortured soul and the quotidian events that need to be negotiated if he is to have a function as a human being – an 'animal with ideas' – lies at the heart of the novel, and reflects a fundamental paradox in the life of the Consul, a tortuous, self-loathing self-portrait of his creator. 'Function' – not at all incidentally – is a word that is uttered with sinister insistence in the closing chapter by the police officer who will kill the Consul.

The novel has attained mythic stature for readers, its fans including numerous writers from Mexico and elsewhere in Latin America, as well as from the English-speaking world, since its publication in 1947, after a strenuous, decade-long gestation.

Despite filmic potential – as a classical tragedy set against a dramatic landscape – it has only made it to the cinema once, in one of John Huston's last ventures, and although Albert Finney's Consul is superb, the film fails to convince in its portrayal of the other lead characters, Yvonne and Hugh, perhaps for the very reasons that the novel fails: they are really not that interesting. Essentially, Lowry was concerned with a single character: the Consul, Geoffrey Firmin.

*

Foiled in my plans for a late night constitutional by the watchman's warning – I tend to err on the side of caution these days – I return to my room. I am a long-term insomniac, and although optimistically convinced that at some point I will 'catch up' on all the sleep I have missed, that rarely happens, and I suspect I will remain in a state of lack for the rest of my days. Instead, I read, drifting in and out of slumber on occasion, a rhythm that especially suits the reading of this book.

At one point, quite early in the novel, the Consul insists, with typical grandiosity, that he is involved in a 'great battle', although he is, at that moment, doing nothing more than discussing whether to go on a visit to the bullfight in a neighbouring town or to stay at home with Yvonne. That notion of 'the battle', the sense of carrying a massive burden, of suffering this great responsibility to 'come through' in a struggle for survival, is drawn upon by the Consul when he resists the opportunity of going home, of calling off the trip, of simply spending some time with poor, exhausted Yvonne. Laruelle, his friend, reminds him: 'you've got her back ... you've got this chance', to which the Consul replies, with magnificent self-importance, 'You are interfering with my great battle' – and again, rhetorically: 'You deny the greatness of my battle?' At the end of this passage the Consul continues speaking, taking Laruelle's part in the conversation as well as his own: 'even the

suffering you do is largely unnecessary. Actually spurious.' But Laruelle isn't there anymore. The Consul is talking to himself. For much of the book, if he is not talking to himself, he is addressing one of his inner demons or 'familiars', which amounts to the same thing.

One of the best examples of the Consul's mind at battle with his familiars appears in Chapter Five, when he leaves Yvonne sleeping inside the house – or so he thinks (in fact Hugh has taken Yvonne riding) – in order to venture into the garden and retrieve a bottle of tequila he has kept hidden in the shrubbery. The chapter picks up on some of the novel's main themes or 'useful debris', in which we find references to film and to cabalistic philosophy, varieties or brands of alcohol, the local geography, horses, flora and fauna, and we meet with dogs, which, in different forms, appear fifty-eight times over the course of the novel. The passage is worth citing in its entirety:

'We warned you, we told you so, but now that in spite of all our pleas you have got yourself into this deplorable – .' He recognised the tone of one of his familiars, faint among the other voices as he crashed on through the metamorphoses of dying and reborn hallucinations, like a man who does not know he has been shot from behind. ' – condition', the voice went on severely, 'you have to do something about it. Therefore we are leading you towards the accomplishment of this something'. 'I'm not going to drink', the Consul said, halting suddenly. 'Or am I? Not mescal anyway.' 'Of course not, the bottle's just there, behind that bush. Pick it up.' 'I can't,' he objected – 'That's right, take just one drink, just the necessary, the therapeutic drink: perhaps two drinks.' 'God,' the Consul said. 'Ah, Good. God. Christ.' 'Then you can say it doesn't count.' 'It doesn't. It isn't mescal.' 'Of course not, it's tequila. You might have another.' 'Thanks, I will.' The Consul palsiedly readjusted the bottle to his lips. 'Bliss. Jesus. Sanctuary ... Horror,' he added. ' – Stop. Put that bottle down, Geoffrey Firmin, what are you doing to yourself?' another voice said in his ear so loudly he turned around. On the path before him a little snake he had thought a twig was rustling off into the bushes and he watched it a moment through his dark glasses, fascinated. It was a real snake all right. Not that he was bothered by anything so simple as snakes, he reflected with a degree of pride, gazing straight into the eyes of a dog. It was a pariah dog and disturbingly familiar. 'Perro,' he repeated, as it still stood there – but had not this incident occurred, was it not now, as it were, occurring an hour ago, he thought in a flash. Strange. He dropped the bottle which was of white corrugated glass – Tequila Añejo de Jalisco, it said on the label – out of sight into the undergrowth, looking about him. All seemed normal again. Anyway, both snake and dog had gone. And the voices had ceased[...]

The familiar speaks to the Consul amid the din of other voices 'as he crashed on through the metamorphoses of dying and reborn hallucinations, like a man who does not know he has been shot from behind.' This arresting image presents the Consul as a man awash in a sea of phantasmagoria, the idea of 'being shot from behind' heavily foreshadowing the novel's ending. Moreover, the brisk discussion being carried out by the Consul with his familiar carries a toxic, comic – or toxically comical – element that will persist over several such scenes. Its insistent, hectoring tone both incites the Consul to drink ('Pick it up'; 'You might have another') and at the same time to back off ('horror'... 'Stop. Put that bottle down'), an argument that the Consul has with himself throughout the first half of the book, after which he is too drunk to care. The snake, cunningly disguised as a twig, appears as a symbol both of the Fall, and of man beguiled by woman. Not, of course, that the Consul was concerned 'by anything so simple' as snakes – and here again we are confronted by the man's grandiosity; he, who has stared into the very mouth of hell (the book has close parallels with Dante's *Inferno*) is not concerned by a mere serpent, and on this account he feels pride, before 'gazing straight into the eyes of a dog', which recalls the ancient Mexican belief that these animals acted as guides to the underworld. The dog is 'disturbingly familiar', which is not surprising as we met this very dog a few pages earlier, when the Consul and Yvonne entered their property on Calle Nicaragua, and its 'familiarity' has an explicit double meaning also. The Consul's reaction to it, too, is identical to the previous encounter, and he utters the word 'perro' (dog) as much in recognition as in description, thus iterating one of the central themes of the novel, that of perpetual repetition, or endless return.

I am not sure if the proliferation of animals in *Under the Volcano* has been given full critical treatment but it strikes me as one of the central features of the novel. One writer who has paid attention is Javier Marías. There is a section in his *Written Lives* in which Marías lists some of the disasters of Lowry's own life as recounted by Lowry himself. The strange thing is that the three stories he tells all concern animals: (i) a pair of elephants allegedly spotted by Lowry and his friend John Sommerfield hanging out on a street corner in Fitzrovia in the 1930s; (ii) the occasion when Lowry, convinced that a passing horse had snorted at him 'derisively', punched the poor creature so hard (just below the ear) that it 'quivered and sank to its knees'; and (iii) the time that Lowry, stroking a pet rabbit with his 'small, clumsy hands' accidentally broke the animal's neck, only to be consumed by remorse, and 'wandered the streets of London for two days carrying the corpse... consumed by self-loathing'.

In *Under the Volcano*, it is when the Consul is at his most lubricated and fluent that the animals begin to pile up in abundance, as in Chapter Five. If this is the case, it reflects that the mind – especially, perhaps, the alcoholic mind – thinks in terms of animals because animals provide a natural metaphoric filter. Animals, as Claude Lévi-Strauss suggested, are good to think with.

The references to animals are almost too many to name, but it is interesting to reflect on the peculiar term the Consul employs to refer to animals: 'people without ideas' (in contrast to his term for humans as 'animals with ideas'). 'Earlier it had been the insects; now these were closing in on him again, these animals, these peo-

ple without ideas.' They include a pariah dog with three legs 'with the appearance of having lately been skinned' (clearly a *xolo*) as well as, in Chapter Five alone, ponies, a snake, a tiger, scorpions, leafcutter ants, Quincey, his neighbour's, cat; (pink) elephants, a lizard, humming-birds, butterflies, ants with petals or scarlet bloom, an unnamed insect (caught by Quincey's cat); a snake in the grass and 'a procession of thought like little elderly animals'; various birds, a bull, three black vultures, a caterpillar, a large cricket (with a face like a cat); a scorpion and some 'murdered mosquitoes'. Indeed, 'the whole insect world had somehow moved nearer and now was closing, rushing in upon him'. Throughout the book flutter a host of birds, in their capacity as omens: in Chapter One alone we encounter 'sleepy vultures'; 'small, black, ugly birds, something like monstrous insects'; 'a frantic hen'; 'fowl roosting in apple trees', and another vulture for good measure. In the book as a whole, I counted 153 references to mammals, insects and birds, and no doubt missed a few.

Lowry's own 'great battle' with alcohol has been well documented, and not least through critical analysis of his masterpiece. He was never able to replicate the success of his singular, most powerful novel, and the reason is clear: he was too drunk, too much of the time. One of the best studies of Lowry and his writing is by the American writer and rock musician, David Ryan. In his intimate, exacting essay, Ryan says that Lowry, like most addicts, never developed a healthy self-identity, remaining wrapped in a state of infantile narcissism. Drawing on Lacanian theory, he claims that Lowry's behaviour as an adult, his mammoth drinking binges and voluntary disappearances suggested an inability to distinguish between himself and the world around him, resulting in chaos with every misconceived utterance and histrionic gesture. That would certainly be true of his Consul, Geoffrey Firmin. And the 'mirror' theme is supported in a couple of anecdotes recorded by those who knew Lowry.

One of Lowry's biographers, Douglas Day, provides an anecdote from an old friend of the author, James Stern, who 'recalled how fascinated he [Lowry] was with mirrors', and recounts one episode at a party when Lowry disappeared, and Stern found him in the bathroom, in front of the mirror, snorting blood from his nose, which he caught in his hands and 'thrust up to the ceiling , so that the whole place was red and white', all the while staring at himself in the mirror and laughing. Lowry's French translator, Clarisse Francillon, remembered his 'habit of slyly watching for audience reaction whenever he was behaving outrageously'.

Among the many photographs of the writer posing, glass or bottle in hand, one shows him holding a mirror, reflecting his own image as he is being photographed; and this inevitably leads to the question: why do so many of the photos of Lowry – including those on the dust jackets of books about him – show the writer shirtless, dressed in bathing shorts, staring at the camera in a manner at once glazed and pompous, trying to make an impression with his meagre moustache and his chest pushed out like a bantam cock, as in the often-reproduced photo of Lowry at Burrard Inlet? Why so many photos of a half-naked Lowry? And when we get past the bared torso and the chest hair and the focus on the face – the one on the back cover of the Penguin Modern Classics edition of *Under the Volcano* – there is something both arrogant and vapid and fearful in those cold, clear eyes. The gaze, we might surmise, is intended to be piercing and riveting, but our attention is distracted by the sparse filaments of the faint moustache, the suggestion of vulnerability in the chin and the plump cheeks, a vaguely satyric pointedness to the ears; in fact what the portrait suggests more than anything else is that the sitter knows that he is meant to be there, but is unfortunately elsewhere, unobtainable, or more likely nowhere, waiting for this to be over with so he can go get another gin. More gin, buckets-full if at all possible, rivers-full, oceans-full of gin. This fantasy, which I am attributing to Lowry, originates in the Consul's delirious outburst in *Under the Volcano*, when he attempts to recall an earlier life in Granada, Spain:

How many bottles since then? In how many bottles had he hidden himself, since then alone? Suddenly he saw them, the bottles of aguardiente, of anís, of jerez, of Highland Queen, the glasses, a babel of glasses – towering, like the smoke from the train that day – built to the sky, then falling, the glasses toppling and crashing, falling downhill… bottles of Calvados dropped and broken, or bursting into smithereens, tossed into garbage heaps, flung into the sea, the Mediterranean, the Caspian, the Caribbean… the bottles, the bottles, the beautiful bottles of tequila, and the gourds, gourds, gourds, the millions of gourds of beautiful mescal… How indeed could he hope to find himself to begin again when, somewhere, perhaps, in one of those lost or broken bottles, in one of those glasses, lay, for ever, the solitary clue to his identity?

Oh, that beautiful tequila and beautiful mescal! The simplicity of the descriptor reminds me of Hemingway's choice of adjectives when writing to his friend Archie MacLeish in June 1957. Having been restricted by his doctor to a single glass of wine per day with his evening meal, he looks forward, with euphoric anticipation, to 'a nice good lovely glass of Marques de Riscal'. This is an impossible utterance in the mouth of anyone except a crazed devotee, but as expressed by a writer who avowed a parsimonious approach to adjectives, the collocation of 'nice', 'good' and 'lovely' must be regarded with deep suspicion.

Malcolm Lowry's grotesque diminution, his descent into the wretched, querulous, occasionally violent individual who choked to death on his own vomit in a rented house in Hove, England – a place epitomising parochial English decorum – represents a pathetic shadow death compared to the Consul's fictional passing, flung down a Mexican ravine after his drunken debacle in the El Faro bar, followed by a dead dog that someone throws after him.

*

It always seemed to me that what literature and alcohol had in common was that they both allowed, momentarily, the ability to perceive things from a place of enhanced perception, or at least to provide the illusion that you were really engaging with the stuff of life at a heightened level. Lowry summarises this clairvoyant state perfectly in *Under the Volcano*, when the Consul attempts to explain to his wife, Yvonne, why he is the way he is:

'But if you look at that sunlight there, ah, then perhaps you'll get the answer, see, look at the way it falls through the window: what beauty can compare to that of a cantina in the early morning?… for not even the gates of heaven, opening wide to receive me, could fill me with such celestial complicated and hopeless joy as the iron screen that rolls up with a crash, as the unpadlocked jostling jalousies which admit those whose souls tremble with the drinks they carry unsteadily to their lips. All mystery, all hope, all disappointment, yes, all disaster, is here, beyond those swinging doors.'

And a little further on: 'how, unless you drink as I do, can you hope to understand the beauty of an old woman from Tarasco who plays dominoes at seven o'clock in the morning?'

I am tempted to compare this passage with Ronnie Duncan's account of a visit to Crete with the Scottish poet W.S. Graham, in which Graham expresses an idea that would be familiar to Lowry's Consul. Duncan is trying to get Graham to come out for a walk, to visit a museum, rather than continuing to drinking himself into oblivion – as he has done every day of the trip thus far – on the balcony of his hotel room:

'So I held on like a terrier and eventually he gestured around the balcony – at the sea, mountains, beach and the tumble of houses on either side – and said that his task was to turn all these into words. 'It is all', he said, 'better than I could ever have hoped' – reminding me that he'd said this on arrival. And then it came to me that there was really nothing else he wanted or needed: this one experience of a Cretan setting, supplemented by visits to some all-Cretan tavernas, was all he could encompass or wished to encompass.'

Lowry and his early morning cantinas, just as Graham and his Cretan tavernas; both of them are relaying an idea that promotes a kind of epiphany – what alcoholics are reputed to call 'a moment of clarity'. Compare 'not even the gates of heaven, opening wide to receive me, could fill me with such celestial complicated and hopeless joy' with 'all he [Graham] could encompass or wished to encompass'. And again, consider this eulogy to Lowry, written by his close friend Earle Birney, and cited in Schmidt's Introduction: '… his whole life was a slow drowning in great lonely seas of alcohol and guilt. It was all one sea, and all his own. He sank in it a thousand times and struggled back up to reveal the creatures that swam around him under his glowing reefs and in his black abysses.' Both Lowry and Graham shared the conviction that alcohol might open the gates of perception. How extraordinary that so much can be invested in an alcohol-enhanced vision of this kind, in which you are – or else *believe* you are – seeing more sharply, engaging more profoundly, empathising more absolutely, feeling more deeply; in other words, it might be said, replicating the aims of great literature.

How well I recognise this joyous, delusional state. During the most intense periods of my own drinking career this was all I wished for: to watch it all, to bathe in it, to sink into the sun-dappled splendour of the world. Perhaps – eventually – to turn it into words. I started serious early morning drinking while living in Hania, Crete, in my early twenties. It had always been taboo, I guess – recalling the story from my schooldays of a boy whose mother slept with a bottle of Scotch at her bedside – but once I started round-the-clock drinking, the chips were in; even I understood what it signified. And for my friend Peter, who lived in a tin shack next door, but who had once lived in Cuernavaca, intoxicated absorption in the beauty of the moment was his creative mission; but long ago he had lost the impetus that originally drove him – to turn it into paintings – and now the drinking was simply an everyday necessity, and he had stopped painting, working instead as a comedic or parodic waiter at the once notorious *To Diporto* fish restaurant in Odos Skridlov, the street of leather, until he was too dissolute even for that place, whereupon I took over the job. How pervasive is this terrible myth among the artists I grew up amongst, the ones I read and admired, the ones whose pictures I watched being made in the Slade School of Art when I was an under-

graduate in London and where I spent more of my social time than among my fellow-students at the LSE; how prevalent this delusion that drink and drugs would somehow help us experience life more 'deeply'. Those raki mornings with Peter, when the morning sun flooded the ramshackle square in the Splanzia quarter, where we lived, with its pots of red geraniums and the sheets hanging out over the railings of the brothel next door, the sounds of the town waking, the glorious sense of detachment too – to be a part of it and yet apart from it – these are the things I felt in regard to both my Cretan and, much later, my Mexican sojourns, until a final, catastrophic visit to Guadalajara put an end to this bright and beguiling fiction...

I am so comfortable in my whitewashed room that I don't want to sleep, and I read almost until dawn, completing the first half of the book, before drifting into fitful slumber. I wake at nine, utterly distressed and worn out, the fan above my head whirring insistently with a regular click at each revolution. Outside there is absurdly loud birdsong, and the sun is struggling to break through thick rainclouds. I drink a coffee, smoke a cigarette, and order a taxi into town, where I have arranged to meet up with the poet Pura López Cólome, Seamus Heaney's Spanish translator, who will be my guide to Cuernavaca for the day, and we will visit Cortés' palace to see the Diego Rivera murals, and walk the streets that furnish Lowry's novel. But already I am less concerned with the reality of Cuernavaca than I am with the one conjured by Lowry in his parallel city of Quauhnahuac. The actual place has been spoiled for me by its fictional double.

Evan Jones
translates Cavafy

King Dimitrios

As if he had never been a real king,
but an actor, he put on a dark cloak
in place of his royal chlamys, and
stole away unnoticed.
        (Plutarch, *Life of Dimitrios*)

Abandoned by the Macedonians –
proof they preferred Pyrrhus –
King Dimitrios (he of noble
character) did not at all – so it
is said – carry himself like a king.
He removed his golden robes,
slipped off his royal
footwear. He dressed
in simple clothes and escaped.
Like an actor who changes
out of costume and exits
once the play is over.

Attendants of Dionysus

The craftsman, Damon (no other more
talented in the Peloponnese), is sculpting
the attendants of Dionysus
in Parian marble. The god leads,
his divine glory, lordly in his stride.
Intemperance is behind him. Beside Intemperance,
Drunkenness pours wine for the Satyrs
from an ivy-wreathed amphora.
Near them, self-indulgent Pleasure,
eyes half-closed, stupefied.
Further back are the singers –
Song, Melody and Revelry – the latter holds
his impressive processional torch aloft;
finally, humbly, there is Ceremony.
Damon chisels this scene. And he can hear
the jingle of the three talents,
his payment, from the King
of Syracuse, a great sum.
Alongside his own savings,
he will live as they do, the delights of wealth.
He may even go into politics.
Imagine him in the senate, the agora.

Footsteps

In a bed of ebony adorned
with coral eagles, Nero sleeps –
self-assured, silent, serene;
his body is strong,
the height of youthful vigour.

But in the alabaster hall where
the shrine of the Ahenobarbi rests,
the *Lares* are anxious.
The small house gods are frightened,
struggling to hide their tiny selves.
They hear a dire noise,
a deathly sound rising in the stairwell,
the clang of metallic footsteps.
Terrified, the pathetic *Lares*
bury themselves in the depths of the shrine,
one after the other, pushing and stumbling,
one small god falling on top of another.
They recognise this sound –
the footsteps of the Furies.

Before Jerusalem

They find themselves before Jerusalem.
Passion, greed, ambition,
even the pride of chivalry
expelled from their hearts.

They find themselves before Jerusalem.
In their ecstasy and devotion
they forget quarrels with the Greek,
they forget hatred of the Turk.

They find themselves before Jerusalem.
And the invincible Crusaders,
often fearless, always daring,
are timid and anxious, cannot advance.

They find themselves before Jerusalem.
They tremble like children,
are tearful like children, weeping,
as they look upon the walls of Jerusalem.

Caesarion

To learn more about the era –
and to pass the time –
I decided to read a volume
of Ptolemaic inscriptions last night.
The tone throughout was of abundant praise
and flattery: everyone brilliant,
glorious, mighty, beneficent;
all their works extraordinary.
If you ask about the women of their line, they too,
the Berenices and Cleopatras, all admirable.

Satisfied with the age,
I would have put the book down but for a brief
and minor entry on King Caesarion
which caught my attention...

And there you were, all impalpable
charm. Throughout history, few
words are reserved for you –
and so I moulded you freely in my mind:
handsome, idealised.
My crafting gave to your face
a captivating beauty and tenderness.
Fleshed out in the depth of night,
my lamp flickering –
how I wanted it to flicker –
you came to my room
and stood before me – as you stood
in conquered Alexandria,
pale and tired, in complete sorrow –
hoping those wicked men might pity you,
they who hissed, 'One Caesar too many'.

Enemies

Three sophists greeted the Consul,
who bid them sit near to him.
He spoke courteously, but soon suggested,
half-joking, they should be careful. 'Fame creates
envy. Rivals write too. You have enemies.'
One of the three responded thus:

'Our contemporaries cannot hurt us.
Our enemies will appear later, newer thinkers,
when we, exhausted, lie miserable
or have even entered Hades. How strange
(and perhaps comical) our methods
and work will seem, because approaches,
styles and trends will change. The same way I,
and so many others, have rewritten the past.
What we portray as beautiful and true,
these thinkers will prove foolish and false,
the same things described (effortlessly) in a new way.
Just as we look in new ways at old things.'

An incomplete history of contemporary German-language poetry

MATTHIAS FECHNER

The history of poetry in German has been embellished with misjudgements. In 1797, Johann Wolfgang von Goethe would graciously advise a gauche and somewhat limited poet, whose name he later remembered as 'Hölterlein', to concentrate on short poems depicting topics of human interest.[1] Gertrud Kolmar, arguably one of Germany's finest poets, was barely published during her lifetime. And Paul Celan's emphatic reading of 'Todesfuge' [Death Fugue] at the 1952 meeting of Gruppe 47 would cause bewilderment among his demure fellow poets.[1] Against this background, it seems a quixotic task to concisely narrate the short, changing and controversial history of contemporary poetry in German, which – due to its lively and provisional character – appears to elude prosaic definitions even more.

Since the patient refuses anaesthesia, let us begin then at one of history's turning points, when the end of an era spread out against the sky over East Berlin's and Leipzig's half-deserted streets. In November 1989, the implosion of East Germany's political system led to a stunning erosion of cultural standards. While the people of East Germany clamoured for advice on market economy, bookstores and wholesalers hastily emptied their magazines to make room for glossy West German guidebooks promising instant success, from house cleaning to stock jobbing. Poetic shelf huggers were shovelled onto the backs of lorries, driven to the opencast mines near Espenhain, outside Leipzig, then dumped into the muddy pits. Verse by Elke Erb (b. 1938) or Stephan Hermlin (1915–1997) could not be incinerated, which would have been more practical. The Nazis had already employed this method of eliminating cultural heritage in 1933, and book burnings were thus considered taboo. Eventually, a horrified West German vicar, Martin Weskott (b. 1951), stopped the lorry convoys, after 200 tours had been made. Henceforth, the books were properly collected and given to charity. With a crippled range, many of the East German publishing houses and most of the state-owned bookstores ('Buchbetriebe des Volksbuchhandels') were next to disappear in the market economy's maelstrom, churned by 'Treuhandanstalt', an agency to privatise East Germany's state-run companies. In the summer of 1990, West German politicians also ventured to close East Germany's famed institute for creative writing, 'Johannes R. Becher Literaturinstitut'. During more than thirty years of its existence, the 'Literaturinstitut' had produced scores of fine poets and proved vital in establishing the influential Saxonian School of Poets, the 'Sächsische Dichterschule'. Among its illustrious alumni, no small number had been active in dissident circles. In marked contrast to the Institute's West German liquidators, they had contributed directly to the East German government's downfall. Hence, the planned closure met with fierce resistance from students and staff, and the 'Literaturinstitut' eventually survived. The rift beginning to divide German society, fortunately, did not extend into poetic circles. In a constant exchange of ideas, even without social media, German poets had successfully been circumventing the Wall. Dissident poets and singer-songwriters, like Günter Kunert (1929–2019), Sarah Kirsch (1935–2013) and Wolf Biermann (b. 1936), had been forced to emigrate to the West but remained in touch with their friends and colleagues in the East; while West German poets regularly stayed in East Germany. Gerhard Falkner (b. 1951), for example, would consider himself a member of the Prenzlauer Berg scene, whereas experimental writer and poet Ronald M. Schernikau (1960–1991) studied at the Leipzig Institute when living in West Berlin. In September 1989, a few weeks before the Wall's concrete slabs would tumble, Schernikau even moved into an East Berlin council flat to defend (his very own vision of) communism.

And yet, East Germany's cultural landscape – with notable exceptions (e.g. Aufbau Verlag) – had almost been eradicated by the 'Epochenwende' (Christa Wolf). Though poets could, if they wished, begin or continue sending their verse to numerous renowned West German publishing houses, like Suhrkamp, Luchterhand, Kiepenheuer or Hanser. Another challenge for East German poets proved coming to terms with the disclosure of files kept by the 'Staatssicherheitsdienst' (or Stasi), East Germany's secret service. By 1993, Christa Wolf (1929–2011), literary figurehead of critical and reformed socialism in the GDR, had to explain to the West German media why she had met members of the Stasi between 1959 and 1962, using the code name 'Margarete'. Worse still, in October 1991 it transpired that Sascha Anderson (b. 1953), a key member of the Prenzlauer Berg scene, had meticulously informed on dissident readings since 1975. In doing so, he had not only betrayed his friends, but had decisively contributed to a shadow literary history, conveniently exploited by the Stasi. In 1978, two years after Biermann had been expatriated, and his spacious abode in Chausseestrasse cleared out, poets, painters and musicians would again find a haven in Ekkehard Maaß' (b. 1951) artist flat in a backyard off Prenzlauer Berg's timeworn Schönfließer Strasse. Maaß, brisk host of high integrity, would serve sumptuous dinners from a gas oven, while up to sixty guests listened to the likes of Uwe Kolbe (b. 1957), Adolf Endler (1930–2009) or Armin Müller-Stahl (b. 1930). And, Anderson, a poet himself, was happy to officiate as omnipresent handyman. Unbeknownst even to Anderson, the Stasi had, playing it safe, additionally planted several minor informers in the meetings and had observed Maaß' living quarters from a conspiratorial flat across the street. After Anderson's role as mole had become public, painter Cornelia Schleime (b. 1953) and Wolf Biermann were thus not shy to award him the unpoetic nickname of 'Sascha Arschloch' [Sascha Asshole].

Several years later, members of the elder generation of poets and writers from West Germany found themselves in a different yet comparable dilemma. Too young for exile during the Third Reich, Hans Magnus Enzensberger (b. 1929), Martin Walser (b. 1927) and, above all, Günter Grass (1927–2015) were struggling to explain why and how they had acted as youths before May 1945. Their biographies were put to closer scrutiny by ambitious journalists like Frank Schirrmacher (1959–2014), whose imagination of fear and conformity was limited to West German affluence. And yet, some of the elderly writers' angrily typed literary reactions did not quite contribute to their carefully tended reputations. Former Waffen-SS 'Panzerschütze' (private) Günter Grass even published the prose poem 'Was gesagt werden muss' [What has to be said] in 2012, which clumsily accused Israel's nuclear policy of threatening Iran and destabilizing peace in the Middle East.

Contemporary poetry in West Germany, however, would generally rather draw on historical influences that stretched further back, namely to Kant, his conception of genius and Weimar Classicism. Hence, a confirmed poet could regard himself (or herself) as favoured by lyric fate, in the tradition of Goethe and Schiller. Trained in other professions (law and medicine), dabbling in several professional and artistic fields (natural sciences, painting, history, theatre etc.), the alpha geniuses of German literature nonetheless had left their mark on Germany's collective memory *as writers*. This also nurtured the assumption that poets, who felt they had sufficiently distinguished themselves among their peers, should not bow to the whims of the market and, thus, prosaic breadwinning. Friedrich Hölderlin (aka 'Hölterlein'), probably the most distinguished lyricist ever to write in German, did not only define himself as a poet, at the cost of forsaking a bourgeois existence, but confined himself for thirty-six years to a reclusive, mentally troubled existence in a medieval riverbank tower in Tübingen. And German literary history has graciously received countless successors, particularly among Symbolist and Expressionist poets. In 1944, the Nazis would put their favourite living poets on a 'Gottbegnadeten-Liste' [List of the Divinely Gifted]. And much later even Rolf-Dieter Brinkmann (1940–1975) and Thomas Kling (1957–2005) attracted criticism that ascribed them outstanding, almost supernatural powers of innovation. [Unlike in the GDR, the belief in a poet's divine election also led to the conspicuous neglect of institutionalized creative writing in West Germany; even though many poets have seriously pursued academic studies, often in the arts.]

The new generation of writers, exerting considerable influence on German poetry since the demise of 'Popliteratur' in the late 1990s, might still have been touched by those antecedents. Monika Rinck (b. 1969), Steffen Popp (b. 1978), Jan Wagner (b. 1971) or Ann Cotton (b. 1982)[3] – to name but some of the most prominent poets – have not attended one of the four (most influential) institutions for creative writing[4]. Their hermetic poetry nonetheless invites to discover literary allusions that appeal to the connoisseur, strawberries in burgundy, in the purified

context of twenty-first-century poetry. After their verse had come to the attention of a broader intellectual public in the groundbreaking 'Lyrik von Jetzt' anthologies (2003; 2008), presenting verse of a new generation, they eventually graduated to their most baffling publication, 'Helm aus Phlox. Zur Theorie des schlechtesten Werkzeugs' (2011) [Helmet of Phlox. On the Theory of the Worst Tool], published by Merve, a small Leipzig company with left-wing roots that specialises in (translations of) literary theory and philosophy (Foucault, Baudrillard et al). As could be expected, the flowerful helmet did not become a bestseller. But it made an impact, serving as signpost on the road less travelled by, which about five dozen leading poets predominantly from Germany and Austria had prepared themselves to follow. And with the notable exception of Jan Wagner's (b. 1971) sensitive nature studies in 'Regentonnenvariationen' (2014), their ambitious poetry volumes primly avoided the bestselling charts.

Simultaneously, since the millennium many poets have gravitated to Berlin, where crucial intellectual exchange, networking, support concentrates. There, lyricists would always have the chance to stage a reading, discuss their work, talk to publishers, other poets, passers-by: at the 'Haus für Poesie' on the red-brick premises of 'Kulturbrauerei' (culture brewery), just off bustling Schönhauser Allee; at the 'Literaturhaus', under the chandeliers of a leafy nineteenth-century villa close to the Kurfürstendamm; at 'Literarisches Colloquium Berlin', in an eclecticist mansion house on the banks of the Wannsee; at the spartan-bourgeois 'Tanzkaffee Burger' in Mitte – or scores of other venues, even in the hinterland, especially the Uckermark, a bucolic refuge for parsimonious artists, north of the city, immortalized in several recent novels and, above all, Gerhard Falkner's (b. 1951) 'Schorfheide' (2019) poems. This situation, in turn, encouraged publishers to increase their presence in Berlin. Germany's most important literary publisher, Suhrkamp, made a headline move to Berlin, under controversial circumstances. By striking contrast, barely noticed even by the intellectual public, a small number of independent poetry publishers also moved to Berlin: Margitt Lehbert (b. 1957) moved Edition Rugerup from Sweden to Friedenau where she edits beautifully designed poetry translations; kookbooks found offices in Tegel, whence poet Daniela Seel (b. 1974) and artist Andreas Toepfer (b. 1971) distribute the most representative selection of contemporary poetry in German.[5] Until recently, kookbooks was struggling for economic survival and one of its poetry volumes even alerted the inland revenue. Berlin civil servants discovered that Tristan Marquardt's (b. 1987) 'das amortisiert sich nicht' [literally: this does not amortise] appeared to have betrayed a lack of 'Gewinnerzielungsabsicht', the intention to realise a profit, prerequisite to run a company in Germany.

Even if Berlin has turned into a creative and career-boosting hub, commercialization, the plainer forms of self-centred communication and rent rises have, at the same time, pushed poetry's economic demise. Bert Papenfuss (b. 1956), one of East Germany's foremost experimental poets, old hand of the Prenzlauer Berg scene, was forced to leave his legendary Rumbalotte-Bar, which he had tended in Metzer Straße, and was priced out of his old flat. Ironically, resistant poets like Papen-fuss had established Prenzlauer Berg's arty reputation which attracted thousands of young, hip, and financially independent people into the neighbourhood. Few of them, however, care to read his hermetic poetry or come to his performances. While this did not elicit any public reaction, self-centred reader response created a major poetry scandal in Marzahn-Hellersdorf, a borough of high-rise flats on the city's eastern outskirts. In the wake of the #MeToo debate, feminist students of Alice Salomon Hochschule, a college mostly offering courses in social work, demanded in October 2017 to have Spanish verse by Swiss-Bolivian poet Eugen Gomringer (b. 1925) removed from the main building's south façade, dominating the exit of the Berlin S-Bahn station 'Hellersdorf'. The poem – 'avenidas / avenidas y flores // flores / flores y mujeres // avenidas / avenidas y mujeres // avenidas y flores y mujeres y / un admirador' – they argued, transported sexist attitudes, equating women with streets and flowers, and made them feel uncomfortable, especially when walking by at night. Gomringer, probably the most important living concrete poet, had been awarded the college's poetry prize in 2011. This entailed to have one of his poems painted on the college's main building, until the next prize-winner would be elected. The ensuing debate on the poem's removal soon generated nationwide headlines, in which public opinion eventually turned against the feminist students, who refused to adopt a more multi-faceted and lenient perspective. Gomringer's poem was duly replaced by new and politically suitable verse, composed by Barbara Köhler (b. 1959). Shortly after, a local property management company mounted Gomringer's poem in illuminated script on the façade of one of their nearby tenement blocks, adding a half-happy ending to an embarrassing discourse. Granted, the students' anxiety seemed justified. But their unwillingness to reflect on and tolerate poetic ambiguity in patinated verse also betrayed an attitude that might not be conducive to the flourishing of controversial poetry (and informed debates). Not surprisingly, a group of conservative poets and writers, mainly from Dresden, has retreated to a position alleging that German society had fallen under the spell of political correctness (even if the Gomringer case might have proved this simple equation wrong). After members of the group had signed controversial declarations on the freedom of speech (2017) and immigration policy (2018), public opinion promptly wheeled left. And Dresden's most prominent conservative writer, Uwe Tellkamp (b. 1968), found himself labelled as a right-wing extremist. Against the background of the 1990 takeover of East Germany, Tellkamp and his comrades-in-arms, poets Jörg Bernig (b. 1964) and Monika Maron (b. 1941), would thus declare themselves victims of a public debate manipulated by West German media. In a highly charged live discussion with Durs Grünbein (b. 1962) on 8 March 2018, Tellkamp emotionally claimed that West Germans once again tried to discredit critical voices from East Germany. German media have, indeed, waged numerous smear campaigns (which included the instrumentalization of poetry: as in the case of a pornographic poem by cabaret artist Jan Böhmermann (b. 1981), read on public television in March 2016, vilifying Turkish president Erdogan as a sheep shagger, and worse). But it seemed to have escaped Tellkamp's attention that his pleading was delivered to a full house in Dresden's Kulturpalast, organised by the city of Dresden, applauded by a sympathetic local public, uploaded by municipal civil servants on YouTube and, this is true, controversially discussed in the media.

As in Dresden, capital of Saxony, Germany's federal spirit and the internet have, in their own rights, contributed to the stabilisation of other regional centres where contemporary poetry has been allowed to flourish. In 1993, 'Lyrikkabinett' was founded in Munich, an institution comparable to London's South Bank Centre, with forty-five readings per year and a library holding more than 65,000 volumes of poetry and other media. Prestigious literature festivals have been held in Frankfurt-on-Main and Bremen ('Poetry on the Road'), even organised by poets in Edenkoben (Hans Thill, b. 1954) and in Hausach im Tal in the Black Forest (José F.A. Oliver, b. 1961). Henrieke Stahl's (b. 1970) research centre on contemporary poetry ('Lyrik in Transition') at Trier University has established itself as a major venue for academics and poets not only from Europe, but also from China, Japan, the Americas and, above all, from Russia. Moreover, most major (and some minor) cities have followed Berlin's example of running 'Literaturhäuser', centrally located in representative buildings, in Hamburg, Frankfurt-on-Main, Stuttgart, but also in Halle and Kassel. Currently, there are 16 Literaturhäuser in Germany, 10 in Austria and 7 in Switzerland – all of them, among other intents and purposes –, dedicated to the cultivation of contemporary poetry. Last but not least, contemporary poetry can also be found on the internet, on 'Haus für Poesie's' 'Lyrikline' site (lyrikline.com), presently offering more than 13,000 poems in eighty-seven languages, many of them in translation, often read by the poets themselves on audioclips. Poetenladen, on the other hand, has expanded from a website into an analogous presence in Leipzig, city of an annual bookfair that comes second only to Frankfurt (poetenladen.de). And anybody interested in current debates and criticism is invited to consult poet Hendrik Jackson's (b. 1971) website lyrikkritik. de and fixpoetry.com.

We might thus end the story, maybe appraising the latest anthologies on contemporary poetry, Steffen Popp's 'Spitzen' [Tops] (2018) and Michael Braun and Hans Thill's more eclectic 'Aus Mangel an Beweisen' [For lack of evidence] (2018). Then close our school anthologies on German-language poetry – 'Echtermeier' or 'Der Große Conrady' – casting a trusting glace at the last chapter, on contemporary poetry. Content that students are afforded the chance to interpret poems by Gerhard Falkner and Ulla Hahn. But, then again, we might consider two final misjudgements.

Firstly, regarded in a broader societal context, poetry as a genre, and especially contemporary poetry, has actually suffered from severe neglect by educational institutions, especially in Germany. Moreover, most German politicians implementing education policies have, in assiduous ignorance, busily been erasing the fading traces of poetry, especially contemporary poetry from their federal school curricula. Admittedly, contemporary poetry has become a major topic in the Berlin *Abitur* (A-levels). At the same time, however, poems are categorized and subsumed as 'culturally significant texts' – in the Berlin curriculum for middle schools. Their treatment in class is no longer compulsory; a provision that mostly affects students with a migrant background leaving school after class 10. In the grammar school curriculum of my home state, Rhineland-Palatinate, which dates from 1998, contemporary poetry is labelled as 'postmodern' literature and Rolf-Dieter Brinkmann mentioned as an exemplary contemporary poet. Brinkmann died on 23rd April 1975 in London, heedlessly crossing Westbourne Grove. In the much-lauded grammar school curriculum of Bavaria, contemporary verse can be interpreted in grade 12 classrooms if they conform to the topics of 'hermetic poetry' and 'developments in contemporary literature'. Apart from the above-mentioned courses at Hildesheim, Leipzig, Vienna and Biel, only a small number of universities offer seminars on creative writing. General studies and orientation years where such courses could prosper have, in fact, been concepts alien to the specialised study curricula of German universities.

Secondly – and more optimistically, contemporary German-language poetry surpasses the areas mapped by anthologies (or, rather, their editors), by influential groups and political geography. Exophonic writers have increasingly been contributing to poetry in German. Accomplished Japanese writer Yoko Tawada (b. 1960) has graduated from insider tip to crowd puller, filling lecture halls at major universities. While Tawada's bilingually tinted poetry might appear as hermetic, her lyric questioning of German language and culture has nonetheless tempted a widespread readership to grapple with her ingenious writings. The success of lyricists like Oleg Jurev (1959–2018), Olga Martynova (b. 1962), Aras Ören (b. 1939), Zehra Çirak (b. 1960), Tzveta Sofronieva (b. 1963) and Safiye Can (b. 1977) – to name but a few – testifies, on the one hand, to the fact that German-language poetry also shows infectious and integrative qualities. On the other hand, the limelight which Romanian German Nobel Prize winner Herta Müller (b. 1953) and her late mentor Oskar Pastior (1927–2006) have enjoyed, seems to out-dazzle other ethnic German poets from Romania or the former Soviet Union. Few of the contemporary Russian German poets starring in Elena Zejfert's (b. 1973) voluminous anthology *Der misstrauischen Sonne entgegen* [*Against the Wary Sun*] (2013) are known even to academics. Major Russian German poets, like Nelly Wacker (1919–2006) and Johann Warkentin (1920–2012), have been treated as nonentities outside their ethnically defined cult following. Even verse in dialect and regional languages – of which there are still many in Germany and its neighbouring countries – generally do not feature in anthologies and literary histories. This situation especially applies to poets who speak German and have, at one time or another, published verse in German, or in one of its regional languages, but have achieved lasting fame in another culture's language. Alsatian Claude Vigée (b. 1921), Luxembourger Anise Koltz (b. 1928) and Swiss Philippe Jaccottet (b. 1925) have all won France's

prestigious Prix Goncourt for their poetry, yet their German texts have – by comparison – hardly been noticed in Germany. The same is true for Lisel Mueller (1924–2020), the only poet from Germany ever to be awarded a Pulitzer Prize, in 1997. Although Mueller did not publish in German, she closely followed societal developments in Germany. An interest that until very recently, when Mueller was awarded the Federal Cross of Merit for her poetry, only a few months before her death on 21 February, had not been reciprocated. But sometimes, great German-language writers and poets need nothing but language itself, an idea of their own destiny and a small, dedicated band of followers to climb the most auratic peaks of literature. Last year, on a soft November night, I ran into Alexander Kartozia and Ekkehard Maaß in Tbilisi, Georgia. Both casually invited me to a council flat on leafy Abashidze Street, where I would meet an elderly gentleman writer, 'Givi' Margvelashvili (1927–2020). Givi's housekeeper had prepared a modest dinner of Khachapuri, pickles and Georgian wine in a dimly lit living room stuffed with books and dog-eared manuscripts. Surprisingly, my host not only spoke flawless German, but soon fell into Berlin dialect, in which he seemed to feel more at ease. Then he told his story: Due to his Georgian emigré family, Berlin teenager Givi had been put into a Soviet concentration camp on the outskirts of Berlin in 1945. There, his father was killed, and Givi, declared a Soviet citizen, was deported to live with an aunt in Tbilisi. Givi soon learned to master Russian and Georgian, but during more than seventy years fiercely stuck to writing literature in German. His stubbornness ensured that none of his works was published until 1991. And consequently, it also established Givi as one of the fixed stars of cultural resistance against the Soviet regime in Georgia, where even Heinrich Böll would pay him a visit in 1972. Givi did not only write dozens of (hermetic) novels in German (and a small number of poems), but also attracted a group of committed Georgian poets writing in German, among them Lali Kezba-Chundadze (b. 1944), Naira Gelashvili (b. 1947) and Vamekh Okudzhava.

A sober appraisal of contemporary poetry in German takes us back to the beginning: it seems nigh impossible to sketch a map of verse, then squeeze the universe into a ball, while we even hear music from a farther hall where slam poets (e.g. Julia Engelmann, Bas Böttcher) and songwriters (e.g. Dirk von Lowtzow, Till Lindemann, Smudo) are singing to the thousands, mermaids and minstrels of the modern world, drowning out the verse of Durs Grünbein and Monika Rinck. But we need not be afraid to wake and listen to the poets' human voices.

The story has not ended yet; even for Sascha Anderson, now married to playwright Theresia Walser (b. 1967), daughter of Martin Walser. As a poet, he has continued to write and publish verse. More recently, he even read his poetry in a Prenzlauer Berg club. I asked Bert Papenfuss and Gerhard Falkner if Anderson's chutzpah made them angry. Surprisingly, they told me they had attended his reading. He had served his sentence, they agreed. Three decades of ostracism were enough.

Notes

1 Goethe commenting in a letter to Friedrich Schiller (23 August 1797) on Hölderlin's visit.

2 Gruppe 47 had been the largest and single-most influential literary group in West Germany, existing from 1947 until 1967. During its 1952 meeting, Paul Celan's reading of 'Todesfuge' was perceived as 'priestly' (Günter Grass) and 'tearful' (Heinz Friedrich). Helmut Böttiger would later clarify that Celan's poetry had been critically appreciated by Gruppe 47; while only his reading style, inspired by Josef Kainz and Alexander Moissi, would cause some bewilderment Cf. Helmut Böttiger, 'Alle Dichter sind Juden'. Der Auftritt Paul Celans bei der Gruppe 47 im Mai 1952. Deutschlandfunk Kultur. Berlin. 21.05.2017: www.deutschlandfunkkultur.de/literatur-feature-vom-21–5-2017-sendungsmanuskript-als-pdf.media.afa78409d62ce194fe7c19b98ed1c9b2.pdf (20.06.2020)

3 This apparently random selection is not entirely arbritrary, as Christian Metz has shown in his essayistic study Poetisch Denken. Die Lyrik der Gegenwart. Frankfurt-on-Main, 2018, focusing on the above-mentioned poets.

4 I.e.: Sprachkunst at University of Applied Arts Vienna (Austria); Institut für Literarisches Schreiben und Literaturwissenschaft at Hildesheim University (Germany); Literarisches Schreiben at Leipzig University (Germany); Schweizerisches Literaturinstitut Biel (Switzerland).

5 Cf. the most recent catalogue of spring 2020: https://issuu.com/kobo_berlin/docs/kookbooks_fr_hjahr_20 (13 June 2020).

The Day After – An Essay
On Sophocles' Farewell To Poetry

SHARRON HASS

Translated By Gabriel Levin

Sophocles has a secret. He calls the secret
OEDIPUS AT COLONUS.

There are different ways to keep a secret. The most common being
heartbreak.

Day after day, at the end of working for eight hours
Nabokov had at best only 175 words.

Nabokov isn't Sophocles. But towards the end
for both of them, like Shakespeare,
heartbreak wasn't good enough

as the secret's most common mechanism.
I'm not confused: this isn't poetry
this is an essay on Sophocles' farewell

to poetry; and nonetheless I'm writing
in short lines with gaps. This is another way
to sit on a rock like the aged
Sophocles.

A short line is far more similar to a rock
than a long line.
It's hard to lie. And not only because of dis-
comfort.

Owing to exhaustion.

*

Twenty years after he wrote *OEDIPUS REX* and thirty-five years
after *ANTIGONE*

and shortly before his death most likely in 406 BC (before Athens
is defeated by Sparta)
Sophocles writes *OEDIPUS AT COLONUS.*

Colonus is a deme in Attica, northwest of
Athens. Sophocles names it 'The white

Colonus' perhaps due to the chalk quarries in its vicinity. There
he was born, in that deme, sacred to Poseidon

The Horse-Tamer. What prevailed over Sophocles when he had his ninety-year-old
hero, his own age, buried in Colonus?

Survival isn't a crime.

Claims the homeless peddler
founder of a peddlers' guild whose emblem is a blanket.

I earn my living from what is most precious to me
reading and writing.

Before summer, in the museum's basement, as we approached
blind Oedipus' departure unaccompanied
into the vanishing fields

we left far behind
the wretchedness of theory,
the reading of what's known beforehand, like
the smearing of the reproductive organs in Greek myths (misquotation from Nabokov)

and there still stood at the end of the field someone
who wanted to poke at Oedipus's body.

At night I didn't fall asleep. My legion of sows
gnawed furiously at the gems I flung
at their feet.

But I write what I write
Not to justify this or that
(even if it isn't possible to completely avoid doing so)

I write in awe and admiration.
I kneel in incomprehension.

I believe with all my heart that writing
proceeds against the biographical.

Perhaps Sophocles also believed
and accompanied his brainchild to the brass
threshold and the pear tree, and shoved him
to the ground –
                    that's called in certain cases
                                        heavens.

*

Can a person love
                    death?
The daughter asks
            the father

                        Yes the father replies *within me abides a love*
                                            of death
please pay attention –
                    nothing else will accept
you

        look
            how many dimensions exist in the world
          how many stars exist in the world
        how many empty lots
                    exist in the world
                            and not one lot will consent to your building
a home there
and death   *is the only thing that will consent*

and you must love this
                        (there'll be a brief struggle for air
             but I know everyone gets over it, successfully)
you're laughing
             but I'm not kidding
why not love it
             it follows that FROM HERE ON
                        I LOVE THE EARTH

I LOVE WHOEVER ACCEPTS

me

                        (Avot and his daughter)

*

Sophocles is considered the 'Golden Boy' of Athens
at its zenith.

What can I tell you about him that you don't already
know.

Unlike Aeschylus or Euripides
he didn't stage his plays in the courts of foreign
kings.
He had a weak voice
and consequently concentrated on writing plays
and didn't act on stage.

'Draw up close and slowly draw away
the wine' he told the handsome boy who served him
in one of the countless
banquets.

He liked young, narrow-waisted
boys   (come on over and we'll fool around)

all the actors were men
I suggest not to forget this fact
which undermines the supposedly soothing, partial symmetry

between the face and the mask.
Women who earned a living
could sit in the amphitheater

but not women who were dependent
on men. They stayed at home.

When Oedipus bursts into his wife's bed-
room, which is now also his dangling mother's
bedroom, she too is a male actor disguised

as the queen, it's best not to forget the complications
for when something difficult suddenly turns easy
and simple – -- --

At the end of *OEDIPUS AT COLONUS*, the exiled king, the blind
beggar, all of a sudden knows how to walk into the grove unaccompanied –

finding the unwavering way, one step at a time
there occurs at the tail-end of complications of blood, fate, and stage directions

a REVELATION

*

The Athenians put their trust in Sophocles.
He served for a time
as 'treasurer' of the polis

and was invited to take part in the expedition to Samos
as a military leader. 7 of his tragedies

survived of the more than 100
that he wrote. More than a 100!

Who doesn't weigh up his gains
and losses morning to nightfall? Who doesn't want
to fool around with narrow-hipped boys?

there isn't a single moment in his biography
(to the best of my knowledge)
in which he could have learned from experience that

Survival isn't a crime

the Greeks, and the Athenians in particular,
effortlessly moving in their insatiable curiosity
from generosity to suspicion and festering animosity
and above all
to the admiration of excellence,

put their trust in Sophocles. His success
was their success.
Even though *OEDIPUS REX* did not take first place
in 425 BC
Someone named – -- -- won

I suspect taking second place
betrayed a slight shock
on the part of the fervent and boisterous and avid for novelty spectators

the hero, the brilliant and great magician
who solved the riddle of the Sphinx by quick

thinking, the Golden Boy of Thebes
from the day of his birth, for no REASON,

                        was chosen
by the gods
                        NOT TO LIVE
– TO SURVIVE

at the end of his life there were many days Sophocles would have been happy to return to and relive

did Oedipus have a single day to which he would have yearned to return to in his past

(I speak with caution since there is no way of knowing when the hour of happiness may be snatched away)

the gods MADE SURE that if he walked backward
he wouldn't have a minute in time
free from TERROR
                        or
  RAGE

but I'd like to venture that the gods didn't imagine that Oedipus
wouldn't agree to bear the burden of GUILT

and that he would forcefully keep apart OLD AGE   RAGE
And TIME

what hadn't been possible until then to separate without the gods

the GUILT from the DEFILED

*

Guilt – I told myself can be carted around it dwells in the blurred intersections,
meeting-places of power: heart, chest diaphragm, liver, mental components, and
courthouses; by virtue of time and inextinguishable rage
it's possible to bear it along
as though on wheels –
defilement isn't a feeling or the interpretation of an act.
Defilement is a fact

that succeeds in overcoming time and to remain unchanged. And it
gives rise to terror because it's contagious.
It's possible to purify oneself from defilement only on account of the gods
who are indifferent to time. *But cleansed of its defilement a body bears the memory of the shock*
from the fact that it refused time.   Defilement can lodge in a person as the awareness or
unawareness of having crossed a forbidden limit.
The gods, perhaps because of their reckless sexual and political intrigues, can effortlessly
identify trespassers with their own eyes, and that eye of theirs nails the person to his
innards. But this isn't so for Oedipus – at the end of his days, at the edge of the grove,
when he seats himself on the rock and refuses to get up

Oedipus understands that his exhausted body is a gift to a place that will agree to receive him

AS A GUEST
AND FOR BURIAL

HE KNOWS WHO HE IS – He can gauge
his own strengths. The significance borne by his words and actions.

He's capable of blessing and he's capable of cursing. He is no longer able to harm himself nor to surprise
himself.

HE IS NO LONGER AFRAID OF HIMSELF.

*

Some thirty years ago I read *OEDIPUS REX* for a course at Hebrew university. We were asked to write a paper on the chorus. This was during the first month of my studies. The chairs were dreadfully hard and leaned to the right, toward a cramped writing surface that dried up my conscious thoughts and orientation in space. The world that opened for me in the books, in the lectures, was immense, and the thirst, industry and panic didn't give me a moment's rest. The 'chorus', so I felt, was like a sort of mistake. Most of the time its words were only vaguely connected, if at all, to what was going on, the sounds it evinced made it difficult for me to hear the voices of the speakers. I wrote that it resembled a rampart of water between the gods and us; something gets through, but what? I wrote that it leaps away from the plot toward some other place, that it is attentive but also impatient, that its place is always too narrow and that it elevates itself in order to have a better vantage point – but of what? The professor marked my paper 90, and wrote that he'd lowered my mark by 10 points because I hadn't cited my secondary sources. I then understood several things. That I hadn't invented the 'wheel'. But that I had the ability to invent wheels. That there are things I wouldn't be able to understand and other things that I'd grasp far better, even though footnotes would never be found for such things. And the professor was right in lowering my mark by 10 points – for I wasn't using the local jargon. But how could he know that I was speaking in a different tongue. I too didn't know. If he'd given me a 100 and spared me the suspicion that maybe I'd stolen knowledge without saying so outright, I wouldn't have known that I had within me the ability to invent and to steal.

*

Other heroes died so young.
Hector, Ajax, Heracles...
Few are the heroes in the Greek tradition
that reached old age. Most of them died in battle
or victorious – on their way home

the ninety-years-old dramatist choses an old king
nearly his own age, a king who left him 20
years ago, back in Thebes, on that dreadful day, on the day
he discovered – he, the homeless,
the deliverer of Thebes from the murderousness of the singing Sphinx –
that not a single day in his life was terrible – *but rather his entire life*
was a form of *theater* – a locus in which all around him
numerous citizens, and this time the gods as well, are spectators
                                                to the narrative

he struggles against
as against a lion or a goddess of vengeance or a clown
and freeing himself from the familiar narrative he releases himself
to tribulations and to form-less time. City-less.
A-polis.

At the beginning of *OEDIPUS AT COLONUS*, Oedipus asks the question

who will receive Oedipus

(not who will receive me)

when is the moment in which we revert to referring to ourselves
as in childhood

in the third person

and without a weird spasm of the name
bound to nothing

*

Suzuki Roshi is lying in bed.
He has no strength left to rise. When the dear student enters, Suzuki Roshi bows his head lightly, and the student
also bows.

              'Don't mourn over me'

Roshi says looking straight into the eyes of the student 'Don't be sorry,
I know who I am'

Is something of the sort similar to what Oedipus says at the beginning of *OEDIPUS AT COLONUS*:

                    Who will receive

me?

Oedipus is frail. He sits on a rock. The air is filled with the twittering of birds (nightingales). Antigone for years accompanying him on the road describes to him the place they've reached. When they left Thebes she was a little girl. Several years have passed since she started accompanying her father, while now and then Ismene her young sister, she too her father's sister, joins them. It's hard to say. Maybe twenty. Maybe. Sophocles is very old, at ninety he again reaches out to the family that bedeviled him all his life. He knows, now before his death, he can't allow or protest against the narrative the incomprehensible gods spun – but he can do something that closely resembles a solution, he can make Oedipus mysterious who doesn't strike terror – he can once again turn him into the subject of a poem, into someone

                    who isn't humiliated by disaster

*

Lyrical poetry is ahistorical, it aims
to stabilize the present moment appearing in the first person singular
with the help of transformation and rupture.
Theater is, I believe, different. It's hard to know where if at all meaning trails off between
the bodies that are speaking. The instability
allows for freedom of movement, a feeling of expanse
a horizon, and even a glimpse as such
of eternity, which for the most part we relinquish but liken to remembrance and yet
without a pause it's impossible to accrue value...

judgment –

and perhaps every so often tragedy will deny us all of the above?

Oedipus stops in Colonus with the help of his daughters, Antigone and Ismene.

The play is fashioned as a triptych, so to speak.
The girls will ruin its compact structure, the way children always
mess up the order. We'll come to that in due time.
I find it hard to move on, or to put it bluntly, I'm playing for time.
The mystery in Oedipus' approaching death is the mystery of a miracle.
And I'm preparing myself for a miracle by all-round abstention,
my refusal to give myself over
impels me to sit on the rock, from weariness
but also anticipation.

Of all the Greek tragedies I'm familiar with, if I'm not

mistaken

this is the only play in which THE HERO DOESN'T LEAVE THE STAGE
and when he leaves, he leaves in order to die.

But he doesn't DIE. He walks into the grove, unattended,
without anyone's help, AND DISAPPEARS.
Is this the blessing Sophocles confers on his hero, the hero
from whom he learned that survival wasn't a crime, but wasn't LIFE either
and who spared him from dying

'when we glanced back
                    we saw that the man was no longer present
and only the king was there
                    shading his eyes as if a horrific sight
had been revealed
that was unbearable to look at.
                         How the man died
no mortal can say...
No fiery thunderbolt was sent

by the god to destroy him
nor did any whirlwind surge from the sea bottom.'

maybe the dark
foundations kindly opened beneath him
for the man was taken away without cause

for grief
or anguish

but by any human standards

a miracle occurred!

Sophocles doesn't want to die as he approaches death. Life blessed him
with everything a mortal can wish for

in the blessings of different goddess, in Athena's blessing
the one who strides to the right of her admirers and protects them from all evil
in Aphrodite's blessing showered to sweet raptures, the loosening
                                                                                of limbs

in bounteous Demeter's blessing, who bestows light even in the dark
in Apollo's blessing, music's benefactor, surrounded by the muses, daughters
                                                                        of memory
and in Dionysius's blessing – he who succeeds in wringing water from rock
the one in whose absence it is impossible to overcome any sort of writing block
the one in whose absence theater is an empty shell and neither the poet nor the citizen
                                                                                    are free

this is a catalogue of blessings that would disarm any Greek hero

what is hubris?
        to believe that suffering   (and the gifts)
won't corrupt me

how is it that these blessings didn't trouble Sophocles
and in creating *OEDIPUS AT COLONUS*
he didn't create its negative and provide a victim
so that the gods – who were never miserly towards the poet –
would persevere in their generosity up to and in the wake
of his death –

No. Something else drives him to accompany the accursed hero
                                right to the wonder-evoking end.

Nabokov, in a reply that concludes the interview he gave to *Playboy*
                                Magazine in 1964:

To be quite candid –
and what I'm going to say now is something I never said
before,
and I hope it provokes a *salutary little chill:*

                I know more than I can
        express in words
                        and the little that I can express,
        would not have been expressed,
                        HAD I NOT KNOWN MORE.

                                (Lake Léman, Palace Hotel)

*

Beautiful, white Colonus.
Here the olive and the bay and the grape are about to bud
and in coverts of their silver-green leaves – nightingales
sing. Like the onset and close of good years
sowed in childhood, in the blessed awakening to life –
so in the play's opening and before its end
the grove   *glitters   holiness   singing*

here the father asks his daughter to inquire of their whereabouts
and the daughter has the all-but-reduced-to-nothing father sit
on a rock
        and a shocked citizen shows up

the daughter has seated the father   in a sacred and particularly awesome place

the father must rise and leave immediately
for the place belongs to those whose name one mustn't pronounce
the most dreadful of all goddesses

Oedipus refuses

he recognizes the place.
It is his plot of land.
Here he will be received – here he will die.

The daughter seats her father-brother on the rock in the grove sacred to the goddesses who avenge the murder of family relatives. A father isn't a relative from their point of view, but a brother is. Certainly a sister. Their loyalty lies with the mother and her children. They are the primeval goddesses who emerged from the earth as the world was formed in the aftermath of a lengthy muddle of pacts and violence in the family. These are the darksome Erinyes created from the blood that spattered on the ground when the little son cut with an iron sickle the sex of his big father.

He who slept with his mother and murdered his father *out of a lack of knowledge*
is led by his sister who is his daughter to rest on a rock in a grove
WHICH IS FORBIDDEN
TO ENTER

does an impure person turn holy when a place is found for him to sit?

And what is the meaning of a riddle *IF NOT ITS REPETITION*

In *OEDIPUS REX* every sentence was a trap
That went and closed in on the king
Right here, in this place, every sentence I utter
Oedipus informs the shocked citizen *will have sight*

but this doesn't necessarily mean that we can behold what he utters

We aren't sitting on a rock
AND WE AREN'T CAPABLE OF UTTERING ONLY THE TRUTH

even the chorus when asked to describe Oedipus leans
its imagination on the rock where he is sitting
and compares him to a promontory battered from all sides by winds and mighty waters

The grove is peaceful. The sleep of the dreadful goddesses hasn't been disturbed.
Like a lizard it isn't possible to distinguish THE REMNANT whose name is Oedipus
from the rock.

But wait till he opens his mouth. For when Oedipus-the-remnant opens his mouth it is
as if the earth opens its mouth, as if the unmentionable goddesses – who with supreme
effort received a second name, The Kindly Ones –
had their faces revealed, the faces
of children who never grew up, and only aged. Just wait for Oedipus to open his mouth
– who'd like to be in the presence of the one whom every word uttered has sight.

Heavy as time that upends meaning, heavy as suffering,
like his rage, like his patience – what by nature has no place, found its place
in turning utterly into sight, and *vanishing.*

Before dying, Sophocles wishes for the last time to exchange gifts:

a moment before Athens defeat in the Peloponnesian Wars
the old poet desires to bestow upon the city that raised him and in which
he sprung as an eternal wonder boy
a vision beneficial to itself, a vision of its own enormous potential
let not the city forget that the pinnacle of the humane is no different from the godly
when the homeless arrived and sought out refuge – the king went out of his way,
he halts the ritual to Poseidon Tamer of Horses –
and defends the defenseless
Theseus legendary king of Athens offers refuge without demanding
anything in return to the beggar who bears with him, at all times, the danger
of a plague – now turned into a blessing to whomever *will receive me*

Sophocles wishes to subjugate
our imagination, as well as the city's,
for we no longer treat ourselves kindly
between dreams-of-delusional grandeur and nightmarish-defeat
we've *forgotten*
how difficult it is to bless – in all seriousness – our birth-
                                        place,
a place that didn't always provide and didn't always defend us

and he also wants to bestow on Oedipus one last gift
he whom he turned years ago into a music-box that sang to the cold
and merciless divine voice

he is about to give back to Oedipus his strength as a magician – and when Oedipus will
perform the final and most difficult of magical acts,
causing himself to disappear from the stage

the demesne of Colonus will turn sacred, the demesne of Athens,
all lands far and wide
And Sophocles will learn to die
  (*WHY ARE YOU LAUGHING? WHEN WILL YOU LEARN TO DIE ALREADY*
Hanoch Levin asks his mother)

*

Greek theater (which in fact no one knows how it came into being and hence I would like to stick to Nietzsche's
compelling version wherein the beginning of the theater originated in the chorus of satyrs, satiated in sexual energy,
crossbreeding between goats and horses and men)

developed in the beginning of the sixth-century BC, at the same time as Athenian democracy. Two inspiring inventions
that needed each other to live.

Perhaps it was the theater, the desired and popular entertainment in Athens that assured the citizens in the most
complicated fashion possible that they wouldn't turn into the rabble. What is the rabble?
Citizens who spurned their capacity to say what they   *really*
                                        felt,
spurned so much and for such a long time,
                    until they can only feel what the majority feels.

And the Athenian spectators knew that the body can discover a great deal but that the laws of the soul were slippery,
errant.

Democracy doesn't shy away from changing moods.
The tyrant asks to stop the wandering of the soul in the wind.
Greek theater was dedicated to Dionysus, the god who was ignorant
of where the spirit might wander with its next gulp.
But in order to disclose the extremity of the mind – the same tales of heroes and heroines from the past were repeatedly
restaged, each time the plot changed, once Antigone was buried alive and her lover took his life; then again, in the
hand of a different dramatist, she celebrated her marriage with Hyman her lover, and bore him a boy.
You understand – things didn't occur only once, and that's that.

Sometimes they did.
But for the most part, they didn't.

The old Sophocles doesn't rewrite *OEDIPUS REX*.
He can't change fate.
He can understand it differently.
There were apparently fourteen plays called 'Oedipus'by
other dramatists.

None are in our hands.
It appears that only Sophocles wrote a play on Oedipus in old age.
A play in which there is a struggle over the hero's body.

It's a timeworn subject. As old as tales themselves,
a struggle over the hero's body.
But it's the first time the struggle takes place while the hero
is still alive, and his body is a wreck.

Even if I'm stalling I no longer have any choice.
I must go back in time.
I must talk about *voices*.
It's easier to talk about sights.
But in the place where everything in the end turns into sight –
the voice is decisive.

Please – someone – I'm need some help.
How does one disclose an open
    secret –

In writing *OEDIPUS REX*
Sophocles created a vehicle, a music box, a shell, a trap
in which the divine hears the human.

Listen carefully.
The audience isn't laughing.
The audience would now rather be at a distance of two or three days
from here, when comedies are staged at the end of the festival,
after the tragedies and the Satyr plays.
The audience would rather be at the moment in which the soul isn't put to test.

But at the current moment there isn't another place.
Sight blocks off all sides.
This is Greek theater –
                    You are seen seeing

Sophocles shuts the audience off from above and from the sides the invisible second side of the shell, the shape
in which the theater is formed

now sight turns into hearing, language into vision

and if for a moment we think that the trap is going to shut down on
                                                    the king

that as spectators we have an advantage – that the well-known *irony* is on our side
everything that's said isn't what is said
when we hear the king say

> I know that you are all ill
> And though ill, none of you is as ill as I.
> Each one of you bears his pain by himself
> And on no other, *but my soul mourns*
> *Equally for the city   and for myself   and for you*

(*OEDIPUS REX*, ll.60–64)

– are we not entrapped as well!

Who can in fact say what he is saying? Will we ever know what our own mouths utter?

How are we going to get out of here?
How is *he* going to get out of this?
Is it possible to get out of this?

We sit on all sides and observe how we are seen while we hear the doubled voice. The king who claims that he is the deliverer is the city's ravager. The king who announces that once he finds the previous king's murderer he will sentence him to exile and death – at that moment decrees the verdict. The king who turns to his wife with affection doesn't know that she is his mother who would have had him killed at birth. Shall I go on? Who wants to go on this way – at first it seemed as if we'd received a gift – we know, we know so much that we even manage to hear how the space contracts, contracts and closes in on the deliverer who is the innocent criminal. And yes, we want to see the disaster reach its end, for we will then be outside of it, outside of the disaster, we'll understand how we managed to slip away, but how will we know, if we ever do escape, if the gift that was given to us by Sophocles is to be in a position of forbidden knowledge, a knowledge restricted to the gods, to a prophet, and to a servant who fled into the hills out of fear. We alone in the company of the gods hear at last how they apparently hear us. We swear by what is most precious to us, curse and swear, love and console, write to the papers, write a play, and all this time, in which we're whelmed with feelings of truth and rage and tenderness –a different pattern is formed, a different note struck, – and if it seems that there is a witness who can sound back to us our words: we're mistaken!

Only poetry and dance can transport us to that strange place in which feelings like pity and fear can undergo purification. What is the meaning of unalloyed fear and what is the meaning of unalloyed pity? The occasions when I was frightened and pitiful were occasions in which I was scared and ended up all hunched over. I didn't stand upright at such moments. I pulled through, because time rescued me. But that fear and those feelings of pity – never left me. They're dormant, and they're only waiting to raise their heads again. If only I let them. How not to let them? Maybe with the promise that the soul can go on wandering

and it is easiest for it to wander
if accompanied by song and dance.

What is the one thing that can endure over time the rollicking laughter of the gods. Can you hear them? They hear our language, our speculations as to what might be the right course to take – and laugh.

We're their theatre.

That's why we're here.

To gladden their hearts.

And they don't distinguish between our sufferings and joys – we seem to them distorted in the same measure. Full of frenzy and destruction.

We wrench ourselves out of shape and they applaud.

How to get out of this?

Only by giving shape to the spell of time is there a chance that the event won't destroy me.

And should I want to amuse myself – and not to give shape? If all I desire in the end is to set up the form-less, the old, the blind, clad in tatters, filthy, looking like a clod of earth from afar,
who strikes the onlooker with terror...

It's impossible to believe how much *it* amuses *them*.

And it strikes us with astonishment.

Only Dionysius has a cult image that resembles the true face of the god.

– the mask.

Perhaps Aristotle was mistaken. Or not. From his description it's hard to grasp what happens to us while we're watching a tragedy. Can fear be purified? Maybe only fear of the fear. But even if he was wrong, lack of understanding is our space, and the error is fateful. For without a lack of understanding we wouldn't be faced with what is unknown-to-us, and we'd be left in a restricted space, delimited by our own size, and in the end at risk of cessation amidst random acts.

*

It's oppressively hot in summer in Athens. It's so hot that you can't see your own shadow and out of fear you want to jump. Hot at least as in Jerusalem. Entirely different gods dwell here and there. In Jerusalem there dwells a god who razed the city as a model of justice.

In Athens there dwelled gods who razed Troy to the ground

(the disaster of a ruined city rules over the Greek imagination)

because that's what they felt like doing –

and the Greeks didn't believe there was a secure way to bind knowledge to action

The gods are opaque. There are those who believed they were so opaque that they must be a wild invention – and burned down, while they're were still playing, the clubhouse (Euripides). There are others who believed they could be influenced, precisely because they weren't rational, and that they could be swayed by great personal charm and gifts (Aeschylus). And there are those, like Sophocles, who didn't trust them at all, but he was a congenial person who preferred not to get into an argument, neither with the citizens, nor with the actors nor the gods. Like the rest of the Greek poets – he relied on his own strength and was fully aware when at the end of his life he created an equation in which the human was just as powerful as the Godly.

It's so hot and there are almost no trees around.

Whoever finds himself to his regret midday under the Acropolis, on the slopes of the Hill of the Muses (there Socrates awaited his death in his cell).

or between Areopagus's enormous boulder and the Hill of the Nymphs (where there now stands an observatory)

needs shade. Shade and water.

There's no water. And scant shade.

For the person on foot, best to stretch out under the olive tree.

The oak's thick shade entices – and the fig tree in its sweet shade
under both the sleep of terror

only under the silvery-green olive is sleep refreshing

the olive

The great gift Athena bequeathed to the beloved city

And I'd never heard before anything of its kind...

> A tree not planted by men's hands, but self-created
> > A terror to the spears of enemies,
> > > Flourishes in this land –
> > The gray-green olive, nurturer of children.
> > > Neither the young nor the old
> > > Shall destroy and bring to naught,
> > > > For it is looked upon by the ever seeing
> > Eye of Zeus Guardian of these Sacred Olives
> > > And gray-eyed Athena.

the elders of Colonus sing when they hear Theseus's promise to offer Oedipus refuge and protection.

The farmers thin out the branches of the olive so that a bird can *fly THROUGH the tree*

when Oedipus grasps that he's the criminal ensnared in a doubled symmetrical trap (Aristotle declared it the most perfect of tragedies because recognition

and reversal occur at one and the same time), which closes in on him until he is completely crushed – he clears out

he trashes his own figure

From her chemise [belonging to his mother/sister Jocasta who'd hung herself]
He ripped off the golden brooches
With which she'd adorned herself,
And lifting them pierced his own eyeballs,
Uttering suchlike words: No longer will they behold such horrors
As he suffered and performed!
From now on they shall see darkly what they ought never to have seen,
And fail to recognize those whom he yearned to know –
So singing, he struck his eyes with raised hand not once but repeatedly.
The bloody eyeballs soaked his beard, and did not cease
To drip clots of gore, and all at once a dark
Shower of blood rained down like hail.

(OEDIPUS REX, 1268–1279)

The perfect music box cracks and the human voice is released from its symmetry,
creates a dreadful darkness it's me Oedipus says and his voice
reaches us alone, the gods turn away,
retreat. It really doesn't concern them anymore,
a deliberate mash-up of one's own figure.

I shouldn't have done it he'll say years later,
in Colonus.
And as it happens in the oldest version that we have, in Book 11 of the *ODYSSEY,* Oedipus continues to rule in Thebes,
he sees and is seen even after he discovers that his wife is his mother. The mother hangs herself.

The day after I completed my lectures on tragedy, something unpleasant happened to me and I told someone who knows how to listen, how was it that someone who's got nothing can rage just like that at anyone who happens to be standing in his way, to curse, to go completely berserk – how suffering hasn't corrupted him, frightened him, and I the merest poof and straightaway I collapse on the floor

and she answered, Your telling me has in and of itself released you to some extent from the imprisoning fear, sit – and write on the rock on which he sits

Sophocles, party to the deep feelings that connects patriotism and honor
to the gods, is cognizant

that the wayfarer knows that he *doesn't exist,* that he's *nobody* or alternately, when the silence is deep and undisturbed, *when he, the traveler, the anchor of time in space – is the chosen*

faced with the overwhelming horror of what time will bring – who is better equipped to deal with the unknown, he who
knows that he doesn't exist or he who knows
that he is chosen

years later Oedipus says I'm innocent
and Sophocles stands by him

how do I know that Sophocles stands by him?
he lets the gods speak out to us – almost without intermediary

might one conclude that in the court of justice innocence can only be determined by elimination? Innocence cannot
be proven, only guilt

Believe me the king says who hasn't reigned for years
even if my father knew that I was his son he'd have justified
the ferocity in which I defended myself and killed him

from a legal point of view he's clean – at the crossing of three roads,
the volatile place in which for a moment
there is a break in the monotonous, the king of Thebes, Laius, thrashes the wanderer with a stick-for-goading-cattle,
and the wanderers in a rage no less vehement than the king's, kills the retinue,
apart from one escort, who gets away

rage and hate and a memory for details distinguish the inextinguishable-
                                                        engine of the heroes
it's impossible to wear them out
even when they take us by surprise in their love, like Antigone, it's impossible
                                        to wear them out
in this they are all too similar to the gods

it's impossible to determine innocence it is only possible to determine guilt
I'm innocent of a crime Oedipus says many years after that
                                        dreadful day

in which he ensnared himself

be kind to your web
footed friend, 'cause a duck
might be somebody's
                mother

Oedipus would croon to his children
a song Merope sang to him, his beloved mother in Corinth

from the depth of *OEDIPUS REX* surges the voice of
the Sphinx, a sort of Delphi-on-wheels
it's interesting how poets create a voice-without-a-voice
the Sphinx doesn't appear in the play and her famous riddle isn't
mentioned, all we learn is that Oedipus was the stranger
who appeared at the gates of Thebes
after he'd disposed of the singing monster, the same harsh songstress,
who'd threatened to destroy the city
nothing more than that

the famed riddle as regards who walks in the morning on
four in the afternoon on two and in the evening on three –
an infant, a man and an old man = a human being

doesn't appear and isn't even alluded to in the play
and in fact we don't have the faintest notion what the riddle may have been

but who'll believe me anyway
I know people who've sworn they came across the riddle
when reading the play and for some reason or another
could no longer track it down

but Sophocles knows how to make things disappear and in doing so to render them
more present

the Sphinx even more than the Sirens, is a peculiar monster
the Sirens entice by promising that they *know everything*
but the Sphinx is intriguing because she knows something in the tongue of human beings
   that they themselves can't manage to grasp –
A monster that's keen on language!
Maybe she devoured children as punishment for not solving the riddle
we have no idea. Sophocles doesn't mention this.

But the Thebans admire and love Oedipus –
there's no one who's smarter and more generous and courageous than him
he's their savior: he's the alien solver of riddles
and there's no need to repeat a riddle that's solved, as a joke
it's necessary to repeat it in a new way

from the depth of the play surges
the voice of the harsh songstress from-which-there-is-no-escaping
and from all around the voice of the Pythia of Delphi, Apollo's songstress,
the priests would translate into hexameters
otherwise Apollo's words sounded like pure nonsense
the play's inundated with voices that human beings try to interpret
while the hero speaks in *all innocence in the doubled tongue*
which in the eyes of the poet emulates more closely than any other the *tongue
that delights the gods*

at the age of ninety Sophocles bands up with the blind beggar
death is a sort of solution in writing, an answer to the question where
hold back
the knife or the dangling light raised over the meshing
of life-literature

does everyone participate in his own death?
And everyone who lives – lives?

'Life was impossible' Suzuki Roshi remarks in one of his lectures. 'But if it's impossible
how can we do it', a student asks. *You do it every day,* Suzuki answers.

Sophocles strides towards his death and leads Oedipus ahead of him. Both of them
are about to turn into life-less and death-less, heroes,
bestowing security and defense to their presumed burial ground.
The Athenians will name Sophocles at his death *'The Accepter.'*

A dreadful voice is heard from the heavens

> ὦ οὗτος οὗτος, Οἰδίπους, τί μέλλομεν
> χωρεῖν; πάλαι δὴ τἀπὸ σοῦ βραδύνεται.

You there, you Oedipus, what are we waiting for
You've dragged your feet long enough!

This is the voice I'd been waiting for. The voice that splits and cracks the consciousness-box belonging to *OEDIPUS REX*. The voice that cancels irony and doublings is the decisive voice. Unmediated – now, no longer the language of riddles and prophecy, but rather in a sort of language that is part intimate and part neutral, and devoid of any particular loftiness, as if the gods had endeavored to imagine how it might be easiest to hear them – almost something casual, scary in its abruptness, somewhat humorous, somewhat childish, like someone calling up to me from the street, Hey, shake a leg, it takes hours for you to get moving.

Palai they tell him, the gods, you're tarrying *palai,* which Aharon Shabtai elegantly translates into Hebrew as 'aplenty' but its literal meaning is 'for a long time'. 'For a long time?' When exactly did he tarry?

For years they've been calling out to him, trying to have him pay attention to the fact that he's been chosen, marked. What hadn't they tried. They made him behave like one of them without his knowledge – like the ancient gods and like the king of the gods himself, the one who'd acted brutally toward his own father and

locked him up in the bowels of the lower earth with his sister. A human monster he understood the language of monsters. They scorched his human tongue to make him reveal who he was. And he fled from them – he mutilated his own body, child of bountiful chance, whose parents sought to kill, like the parents of the gods who wished to choke their own offspring. For years they've been trying to get him to understand, and now, only now, when he penetrated into the sacred grove belonging to the goddesses whose name is past bearing, whose revealed name is the Kindly Ones, he understands. The darkness is a way, the light is a locus. We called and called you the gods said – we gave you a sign from the day you were born, injured, risible, lame, come to us

there is no longer a doubled tongue in Colonus. We've reached a place in which the language says what it intends to mean. Now it is the body that turns incomprehensible, deceiving, fleeing from failing strength to strength, loved, bathed by the daughters, only by the daughters, his stink removed by the daughters

what is it that you most despise the interviewer asks the aging Nabokov

to stink, to steal, to torture

answers the writer *without a moment's thought*

and what is paramount in your eyes

to be generous, proud, fearless

Nabokov again replies, who one day, after searching for hours in the woods for a rare butterfly that got away, burst into inconsolable tears

Oedipus consents to move to a rock abutting the grove of the Kindly Ones.
It is forbidden to speak in the sacred grove.
And he persuades the elders of the place to call the king.
They're stricken with terror when they hear that the stranger who penetrated their territory is Oedipus.
And later, with the sort of cruelty that is for the most part untypical for a chorus,
they'll force him to recount his life story,
even though they're familiar with the tale.
But there is a price to cruelty: they will hear again of his *innocence*

When Oedipus returns to the grove of the dreadful goddesses
similitude is revealed to him

nothing ever resembled him
the dreadful Erinyes, the Kindly Ones without whom the earth wouldn't be blessed
those deprived of shedloads of blood revenge in the name of the city and of judgment
out of agreement and persuasion
are turned into goddesses of blessing and mercy, as long as they're granted honor and assured patrimony

the grove opens and (nearly) ends the play.
These are the gods in whose absence suspension, limit, form are impossible
these are the gods in whose absence it is impossible to feel self-worth,
potency and value not toward the human! But toward the powers
that honored him enough and to spare until he felt they'd crushed and left him empty-

handed. And here he is, in the place in which a miracle
of impersonation occurs and he can see himself at last with distinct
features, framed, illumined
dead
a place where he is contaminated
because we, on the outside, cannot help thinking in terms of limits and surfaces
envisioning in the death of irony and the mysteries of the doubled tongue...
and innocence, innocent as if still unborn

he who staunchly stuck to the laws of the city and the gods – which didn't help him
as if he were weight-less   face-less   origin-less

the reach of the play, the middle, the sprawl – there is nothing there that is of the
                                                                                    Godly
if the extremities are gods in order to set a limit and give shape
the middle-range is the deed and the value
for love is deed
and generosity is deed
and rage is deed
(the rage, the rage that seeps through the same megathumos,
big-heartedness, of the heroes)
and entreaty is deed
and all of them aspire to a purpose
while the deception and the torment have perhaps a small, awful aim
– but they are without purpose

at this level of the play
of the big question 'who will receive Oedipus'
Oedipus blesses and curses – like the Erinyes, like the Kindly One
he blesses Theseus and blesses his daughters and blesses Athena

and curses Creon who tries to force him to return to Thebes
and personifies in his dead body
a blessing to the city without the honors of burial
and he curses
his son Polynices who will slay and be slayed by his brother Eteocles
sons who didn't take care of him during his years of wandering

and during the entire length of the play our eyes are fixed on Oedipus, on the grimy
                                                                                    figure
resembling the gaping earth,
and only once
does the play glance away from Oedipus and fix its eyes
on the children
on Antigone and her brother Polynices

Oh Antigone – who are you
you who struggled to alter what the Greeks refused to alter
the principle that one should recompense friends and penalize enemies
and you pleaded with your father to listen to the entreating son
and you pleaded with the oldest son to cease fighting against his younger brother

even your father-cum-brother found a place where he could sit for he found
                                                    that which resembled him,
but you Antigone?
You're destined for the future tense and the future tense
Sophocles has already buried in the past

in every version known to us of the story of Thebes
The mother, Jocaste, hangs herself.
For a mother there hasn't yet been found (since then) the *similitude*

I saw [Odysseus recounts in the Phaeacians' palace in Book 11 of the *ODYSSEY*]
the mother of Oedipus, fair Epicaste [= Jocaste],
Who performed a misdeed in *ignorance of mind,*
Wedding her own son, and he, after slaying his father, wedded her,
Which the gods straightway made public among men.
He dwelled in splendid Thebe, Lord of the Cadmeans,
Riddled with anguish through the gods' deadly counsels,
And she went down to the cruel gatekeeper's House of Hades,
Fastening a noose on high from a lofty beam,
Overcome by her sorrow, but for him she left behind untold
Anguish, as many as a mother's Erinyes bring about.

(Lines 271–280)

Years pass, at least three hundred, and time which upends meanings, as fate, endows the Erinyes prodigious mercies, and sets Oedipus within their precinct, in the grove, as a suppliant awarded refuge, and only the mother's legs dangled in the wind over the earth, her head not in the skies

the mother, Jocaste, in *OEDIPUS REX*, was prepared for a play that no one dared imagine, neither among the heavenly gods nor among the chthonic gods, when she realizes her husband is her son, she asks him to desist from investigating the murder of the king, her former husband, if Oedipus will desist, she, Jocaste, you understand, would be willing, in order to defend her children, to go on presiding as queen alongside him whom she now knows is her son, and to pretend, to hold up a mask, further and further into the future, that he is her lover, her deliverer, the precious father of her children and as long as – -- --

Writing, I tell myself, doesn't aspire to silence
         it aspires to prolific speech, which is impossible
to the by now unacceptable, to the unknown

to what is beyond our strength

and at the last minute Sophocles shatters the marvelous structure, the seductions of
mystery and glorious exalted death of the last bourne,
with the help of the girl, Antigone

the children never manage to keep their shirts clean,
a floor without crumbs
the wondrous triptych is a grove – the human parameters – a grove
    is contorted

where are we?
Antigone refuses to remain in Athens,
The guest of the generous Theseus, exemplary
ally,
she returns to Thebes, to the war raging between her younger
and older brother

Sophocles wrote *ANTIGONE*
some thirty-five years before *OEDIPUS AT COLONUS*
in view of the play's strength Sophocles not only took first prize in the great Dionysia,
but was chosen as well to sail as a general
and quell the rebellion in Samos

the Athenians knew no greater honor than serving the polis,
than assuming responsibility,
than loyalty to one's birthplace
Socrates awaits his death,
in his cell, on the Hill of the Muses
it's only a coincidence, the genial optician tells me
                       close by the Acropolis
but Socrates will refuse to go into exile
there is nothing worse for certain people than to be city-less

Sophocles
knows that he is about to die and sends Antigone to her future
which he already wrote so many years ago

does he assume responsibility as such for his actions – and having no other choice
agree in a state of shock to that which can no longer be altered

does he thrust it into the eternal slipknot of his work
as if telling us –
my work is sealed and autonomous – a law unto itself

or does he create a palpable defect, as a wound
and looking at Antigone from behind retreating
we behold *his shame, his deep regret*
One must save the children
why do we fail again and again in saving the children

Sophocles knows that he is about to die
his freedom was always a secret
and he buries it
In the safest place, in the hideaway
laid bare to the eye
in *OEDIPUS AT COLONUS.*

Notes

From *OEDIPUS AT COLONUS:*
Page 17: Line 3
Pages 21–22: Lines 1648–1665
Page 41: Lines 694–706
Page 49: Lines 1627–28

Page 7: Avot and his daughter. Avot Yeshurun (1904–1992,
leading Modernist Israeli poet. His daughter Helit: translator
and editor of major literary periodical *Hadarim.*

Page 29: Hanoch Levin (1943–1999). Major Israeli dramatist.

Reviews

At Odds with Things

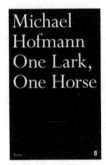

One Lark, One Horse, Michael
Hofmann (Faber) £10.99
Reviewed by Oliver Dixon

The title of Michael Hofmann's
latest book of poems, derived from a
joke told by Primo Levi about a
delicatessen-owner who sells 'lark
pâté' but adulterates it with horse-
meat at the rate of one horse for
every lark, seems to speaks of
ridiculously unbalanced compro-
mise, of a fraudulent world in which
everything sold to us as precious or
specialised is nearly all composed of
cheap, unpalatable stuff we wouldn't
really want. This might include
poetry itself (signified by that
Shelleyan lark), an apparently
rarefied delicacy that's actually a lot
more earthbound and gristly than it
may seem. Levi's joke is apt too
because of the double-speak
inherent in its terms: larking and

horsing around are what jokes do,
after all.

One horse, one lark: two disparate
things, one big and one tiny,
comically aligned. This *Laurel and
Hardy*-like image ushers in a set of
poems which are logjams of objects
and entities in odd juxtaposition,
build-ups of thingliness that are
nevertheless far from Rilke's
'sachliches Sagen' with its aspiration
to capture the inner essence of
phenomena. In the disenchanted
landscape of Hofmann's poetry,
thingliness has become the chewy
horse-meat of an ersatz culture that
purports to have lark-like qualities,
blocking off any sort of lyric impulse
or consoling epiphany, breaking
syntax down into ungainly invento-
ries of noun-clauses and names. Any
more than for Stephen Dedalus on
Sandymount Beach, the *nachein-
ander* of one-thing-after-another
leads not to revelation but to the
rueful hindsight and stock-taking
which characterise this collection,
Hofmann's first volume of original
poems for almost twenty years
(initially published as a hardback in
late 2018, Faber have now issued a
paperback version, which is the
occasion for this review).

The long hiatus, during which
Hofmann published translations of
Gottfried Benn and Durs Grünbein

as well as a plethora of significant
German novels, seems to have
triggered a shift in style away from
the caustic, tightly-parsed quatrains
and other stanza-forms of his earlier
volumes and towards more sprawl-
ing, cumulative list-poems and
montages, often extending over
several pages. Words themselves
have become things, applied in
thick, impasto layers to form what
Montale called 'a counter-elo-
quence'. There's a rich, malty
viscosity to the vocabulary, which
(like the words scratched into
records in 'Lisburn Road') emphasis-
es this materiality of language: 'thick
textures, odd combinations, words
and turns that are both concrete and
collusive'(this is Hofmann, writing
about his own poetry in 1999). Dense
patterns of alliteration and asso-
nance bind together the imagery in a
poem like 'November':

Crows on oaks and cranes and
cooling towers, / the sky cracking
up, and crows investigating / the
cream of whatever crust cracks
yellow

The things in Hofmann's poems are
also markers of time and place,
bulwarks against the depredations
of history and aging. 'On Forgetting'
meanders through the linguistic

amnesia of late middle-age, where words slip from their signifiers, wobble in and out of focus or coagulate into each other. Exasperated by the scatter-brained internet-culture in which he finds himself, the poet contemplates, out of a magpie jumble of references (e.g. Hofmeister beer, Bob Dylan, Bruno Schulz, Jonathan Swift), what little he can still retain. Aging is a recurrent concern, met with disabused resignation and in 'LV' an appalled, poignant disbelief that life could have come to this: 'The years of no impressions and little memory... The years of the unbeautiful corpse in preparation.'

Despite his career as a prolific translator and an inveterate denizen of abroad (as demonstrated by the range of international locales the poems evoke), Hofmann remains a rather British poet in flavour, in so far as his is a social poetry largely impervious to metaphysical flights or any gesture towards transcendence, untouched by the 'cosmic gruntledness' of Ashberian post-modernism. (Or, as Hofmann depicts his own poems in the preface to his Grunbeim volume, 'small-scale, occasional, personal, wincingly witty, articulate about dirt'.) A lugubrious empiricism prevails, perhaps influenced by Hofmann's extensive work on modernist novels: many poems summon up specific locations from the author's past without giving us the story of what happened there, only hinting at a series of 'chaotic exits' and uprootings, including (in plaintive pieces like 'Motet' and 'In Western Mass.') marital breakdown. The theme of not belonging, summed up in the childhood memories of moving to a dismal provincial 60's England in 'The Case for Brexit', is often brooded over, even in the poem 'Derrick', whose terse sketch of an unremarkable neighbour culminates in the reflection: 'more local connections / than I'll ever have.'

The closing poem 'Idyll' envisages a 'post-human' scenario where only objects remain, infused with traces of habitation but ultimately outlasting their owner, the poet finally (in the words of a previous Seferis epigraph) 'not at odds with things'.

A Longer Connection to the Land

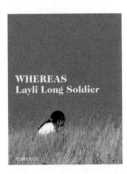

Whereas, Layli Long Soldier
(Picador) £10.99
Reviewed by Evan Jones

The Picador edition of Layli Long Soldier's 2017 collection is physically pared down from the American release, using the same typeface in a smaller font size with tighter margins. It's a dense book and to approach it in this form is a disservice. At least, here, the cover image is fuller, a still from Brian Jungen and Duane Linklater's 16mm film, *Modest Livelihood* (2012). The title refers to a 1999 Supreme Court of Canada ruling that First Nations' hunting and fishing rights are valid only for the earning of a 'modest livelihood' and not for the accumulation of wealth. The still features Linklater, an Omaskêko Cree artist from Moose Cree First Nation in Northern Ontario, sitting in a field of long grass.

Most readings of *Whereas* are attuned to the link between person and language – but the connection to landscape completes what is a trinity: '*I don't trust nobody / but the land* I said', Long Soldier writes in 'Steady Summer', and continues, 'I don't mean / present company / of course / you understand the grasses'. Language, its difficulties and failures, the colonialization of one language by another, the split between mother tongue and the words of the oppressor: Long Soldier critiques the etymologies and archaeologies of the words she uses – always coming back to landscape.

There is a tradition here, linking land, people and language. It is a part of the process of nation-building and *Whereas* begins as a critique of what America is. Long Soldier tells us at the outset what is important: 'Now / make room in the mouth / for

grassesgrassesgrasses.' This invented compound word carries a lot of weight and evolves as one reads deeper into the book ('deeper' in multiple senses, I mean). It is a critique of Whitman's vision of the connection to nature, initially, where it is the leaves that are plural and the grass singular, individuals sighted in the wide-ranging but exclusive democratic field. Long Soldier changes this. The grasses are now plural, there are different fields and different nations. She ends another poem in the first section, 'Edge', with: 'And I see it I Mommy the edge but do not point do not say *look* as we pass the heads gold and blowing these dry grasses eaten in fear by man and horses.' The grasses are a difficulty not a solution, their multifariousness is dangerous. Whitman admitted something similar about the taking up of his vision, issuing challenges to his readers in poems like 'Whoever you are now holding me in hand'. But there is also an insistence on reward in Whitman: an edification, and a problematic utopian vision. Though admiring of Native Peoples of America, he ultimately believed they would become extinct. His late poem, 'Osceola' (first published April 1890), is often cited to reflect this. A leader of the Seminole in Florida, Osceola died imprisoned by the US government. Whitman owned a copy of his portrait by George Cable and told Horace Traubel, 'he was basely betrayed, imprisoned and literally done to death'. The poem describes his last moments of freedom, his preparation for war, and is sympathetic. But it positions Osceola firmly in the past, final, heroic, a victim of Manifest Destiny.

Long Soldier writes about the living. She imparts wisdom to her reader via the stories of a people with a longer connection to the land beneath her feet – without nostalgia – who vie against the hurtful modern nation. In 'We', she writes: '... You and I are not *we*, correct. And for you I have forgotten why|ants in a line dispersed from a singular breath.' She reflects the Wordsworthian 'out of tune', but not by choice. It is the other, the Anglo-European tradition perhaps, that has forced this disconnection.

'38', the final poem in the first

section of the book, tells the story of the Dakota 38 – 'thirty-eight Dakota men who were executed by hanging, under orders from President Abraham Lincoln' on 26 December 1862, following the Sioux Uprising. But it is much more than a retelling – and much more than Whitman's portrait of Osceola. It is the living history of a people, a reminder of ongoing suffering, even as Long Soldier admits, 'Keep in mind, I am not a historian'. She continues:

One trader named Andrew Myrick is famous for his refusal to provide credit to Dakota people by saying, 'If they are hungry, let them eat grass'.
[...]
When settler and traders were killed during the Sioux Uprising, one of the first to be executed by the Dakota was Andrew Myrick. When Myrick's body was found, his mouth was stuffed with grass.

The next line, 'I am inclined to call this act by the Dakota warriors a poem', sums up her position. Here is an alternative to the narrative of the nineteenth century, the weight of Whitman acknowledged and pushed past, the grand American narrative rebuked. Long Soldier reminds us in the twenty-first century that the vision of a united America is just that – one vision. The costs and the losses, the plurality of identity and language and land must now be addressed. *Whereas* is part of that process.

Three Books

The Caiplie Caves, Karen Solie (Picador) £10.99. *Marine Cloud Brightening*, Medbh McGuckian (Gallery Press) €11.95. *American Faith*, Maya C. Popa (Sarabande) $15.95
Reviewed by Ian Pople

On a very obvious level, these are three books with three very varying

forms of address. For Karen Solie, the narrative of these poems is very often couched in a third person, past tense. That grammar establishes the sense of history in the poems, but the direct, uncluttered nature of Solie's writing means that the history, itself, is very alive. Medbh McGuckian is, perhaps, sometimes pigeon-holed as a writer of a kind of *ecriture feminine.* That writing often uses a simple present tense, the effect of which is to present what might appear to be somewhat mystical states and statements, very directly and forcefully. With McGuckian, you get the idea that sentences and actions are one and same; the writing *is* the state. Maya C. Popa's debut volume, *American Faith,* falls between these two writers; sometimes there is a present tense directness in which process is enacted. And sometimes there is a narrative, usually of a very personal kind, which the reader is invited to share.

Karen Solie's *The Caiplie Caves* is a large compendious book weighing in at some 120 pages. At its centre is the story of St Ethernan, a seventh-century Irish missionary to Scotland who retreats to the eponymous caves to decide whether to pursue a communal or a solitary life. On that level, the book offers a reimagining of a life lead some thirteen hundred years ago. But Solie threads through the book other narratives. One such is the story of St Enoch, a sixth-century Scots woman known in early life as Thaney. In the poem 'Origin Story', Solie gives us the tale of Thaney's pregnancy and her father's attempts to kill and then banish her. Thaney washes up on the shore of Ireland where she gives birth to her son, Kentigern. Enoch and Kentigern eventually returned to Scotland where, it is attested, they founded Glasgow; where there is now a square named after her. Solie's vibrant retelling of this story is full of anachronisms, as in this early depiction of her father's violence:

Thaney was thrown from the 25th-floor balcony / of Traprain Law by her father, Loth, / a pride-based thinker / consumed by a tyrant's bloody melancholy.

Those last two lines give a sense of

how Solie might move an idea, and the way the language is impacted and darkened in such moments, where Solie reaches out into a version of contemporary politics. Later, in the same poem, as Thaney drifts out at sea in a coracle, Solie writes:

How long was she out there. An era, floating / in a cortege of unhelpful sea life, // in the imagination of a culture / with a fetish for suffering, / condensed to a bright concentrate / like the picture on an old tube television, // stove inside her, bulb on a cord. / Were she extinguished, it would glow / a little while, not long.

There is the refusal to use a question mark in the first line. And its answer, a long sentence with no verb in which the participles both past and present float as Thaney floats. Solie invests considerable, adroit violence into that word 'stove'. The whole extended metaphor seems particularly apt, even if anachronistic. This is technical achievement of the highest order.

Elsewhere, Solie can be more personal and a gentler, perhaps softer, side to her writing is present:

My love, who negotiated with a Silk Cut / in his wheel hand the unfamiliar roundabout // to the A915 at Kirkcaldy, sweeps droppings / from the paved deck, like an owner, with his whole heart. // He grew old not thinking about himself.

Where Solie's 'fictional' writing allows her to spin away and mine contemporary relevances, her personal, autobiographical poems are a place for quiet celebration and a greater sense of belief in slighter, less obvious human virtues. The poems about St Ethernan and St Enoch are contemporary explorations of faith and its difficulties. These difficulties are located in the sixth and seventh-centuries, but Solie establishes their relevance not simply through the anachronisms she uses both as metaphor and undergirding. The relevance of these early Christians is that their own struggles with faith are not simply like ours but that they point to the difficulties of faith, full stop. Faith in her lover is easier as it is immanent. Faith in God is contingent and based on a trust which the humans around you can wrest and stain.

Marine Cloud Brightening is Medbh McGuckian's sixteenth book. And, as ever with McGuckian's work, there is a range of poems from those in which the narrative is clear and accessible and those in which the trajectory of the poem is something that has to be reached into. In this kind of poem, the juxtapositions may need to be lived with before the emotional and intellectual resonances and refractions emerge. McGuckian is not, in that sense, a L=A=N=G=U=A=G=E poet. McGuckian's project, as I understand it, is to yoke deeper and less obvious connections into a mesh on which the language of the poems rest.

The book comprises four sections of which the second is labelled 'in memory of Seamus Heaney'. The first of these poems, 'A Pauline Verse', runs through all the words available from the words, Seamus Heaney, for example:

> From ash to Ashe // and ashes to ashen, assume to aum. / From ease to easy, eheu and emu. / From ham to hay to hey to hen, / from he to hue to hum, human // and Hume.

This is a tribute not only to Heaney's own fluency but also to Heaney's ability to reach for the deeper connections; as McGuckian puts it in the poem, 'Gold Toad': 'Will you be able to keep coming forth / from the place we have not yet learned / to find a voice for?' This, written after Heaney's death, suggests that Heaney's poems do, indeed, still speak to us; Heaney's voice so original and searching that it speaks where others cannot.

McGuckian has been compared to Ashbery, a disservice to both writers. It is true that both often appear to explore meditative states of mind. McGuckian, however, has made it almost a badge of honour to be more 'domestic'. There is, perhaps, rather less of that in this new collection. One of the poems, 'The Decision to kill John', is a plain, unvarnished account of the killing of an elephant called John, who has gone feral and killed one of his trainers. The date is given as 1927. This poem shows not only the range of McGuckian's technique, or interests, it shows just how widely her imagination runs. The use of the 'Christian name' John for the elephant and its careful, poignant positioning in the poem also shows the range of McGuckian's emphathies. There is much in this collection to satisfy those for whom McGuckian has always offered an immersive, rich poetic experience.

Maya C. Popa's *American Faith* is a very interesting first volume. Not only is there that title, which works both ways, i.e., that there is a faith invested in America, and also that there is a particular type of faith located in America. And then there is the cover which shows a man, back to the camera, drawing a line in the gravel below him with a stick, the line recedes to the back of the picture. Thus division in that 'American faith' is signalled by the jacket of the book. And division is something that is explored on almost every page of this book. But Popa does not explore division in the explicitly ethnic manner that is explored in many other recent books of American poetry. Popa's exploration is very carefully internalised, to see the ways in which division is refracted through the deeper emotions of someone whose background is that of an immigrant growing up from childhood in a new world.

That sense of a faith invested in America, its life and people is questioned on almost every page of this book. Writing up a summer camp, in the poem entitled, 'Elegy: M.C., 1988–2003', Popa writes about the narrator's (it's quite clear, really, that it is Popa's own) reaction to the news that one of the camp members is dead, as she frames it: '*Boy, 14. Dead. Abuse.*'(Popa's italics). Firstly, Popa comments, 'I'm waiting for a cue on the "adult reaction" // but devise it on my own, crying within sight // of a crush to invite his comfort', and below this, 'A new world, // I don't say, not knowing what I mean, // what it will meant to me years from then. // No easy elegy for the one you didn't, // all things considered, work to befriend…'.

What Popa offers here is a focussed examination of how the death of this boy ripples out into the emotional environment. The child who, in some senses, is 'closest' to the dead boy is waiting to observe the correct way to react from the adults. But the adults do not, or actually cannot, provide that model. So, the narrator/ Popa must learn to react in their own way, as though there was a closer relationship to the dead boy than there actually was; a closer relationship which offers agency to the dead, inviting the dead boy to comfort the living. Then, Popa pushes out the implications to the child's sense of the whole new world. That new world, as an immigrant to America, the child can see has implications for the whole of its growing up. That growing up, too, becomes circumscribed by the child's own inadequacies and, to some extent, guilt.

I have spent some time in teasing out Popa's lines because the book constantly invites that kind of attention. In part, that invitation comes from the unadorned surface of Popa's writing. That calm surface contains a precise musicality which Popa quietly modulates to her subject. 'Sashimi', for example, begins, 'I served my loves' sashimi hearts / on iceless beds of clean bamboo. / Some were tasteless, others, / spoiled at the oil rig of our departure. / There was the horse mackerel / bucking at the rice, as if another life / were to await'. Again, Popa carefully moves the reader through the food items; the adjectives, 'iceless', 'tasteless', 'spoiled' leading us through the emotions that the food conjures, to that image 'the oil rig of our departure'. Clearly, there might be a wide range of meaning attached to 'oil rig'. One might be that they've simply spoiled the food with too much dressing. And that might just be too bathetic, but mixed with that bathos is the sense of hugeness, of the oil rig as some huge structure which is somehow stable through whatever is the reason for their 'departure'. Then that splash of imagination contained in the 'life' of the horse mackerel.

The final poem in the book is 'A Technique for Operating on the Past', a poem which has already won prizes. This is an elegy for her brain-surgeon great-grandfather, who had to flee the KGB by 'escaping across / the Carpathians dressed in peasant clothes'. And who 'Like all the men in my family, he was a close reader and musician.' Part of Popa's technical success is contained in the way she titles her poems and the way that title will wash through the poems. Thus, in this poem, there is the sense of the close reading of the brain and its parts as almost a musical act, the interpretation of a score, composed in the past, but re-enacted in the various presents the brain is party to. This is also a score which has political implications as her great-grandfather is able to understand, 'the officer's parietal lobe where his punishment // waited to be articulated, its obstinacy illustrated by early phrenology / by the silhouette of a ram' and that he knows, 'that engine of ephemera could be a sentencing, a silence or a song'. Popa articulates not only the achievement of her grandfather, but also the poetic resonances of his life and time. These resonances Popa sets out with a calm, involving inevitability that embraces both the range of the subject matter and the range of her emotional engagements.

Mutton Rolls

Mutton Rolls, Arji Manuelpillai
(Out-Spoken Press) £7
Reviewed by Joe Carrick-Varty

At one moment darkly funny and insightful, the next prophetic and gut wrenching, the poems in Arji Manuelpillai's debut pamphlet *Mutton Rolls* oscillate between a multitude of tones, as in 'nominated for a BAME prize' when a speaker remarks: 'it's always in capitals / like someone is shouting it', before returning home: 'tomorrow when I

meet my family / I shall tell then I was loved'. Public and private lives, inner and outer worlds, Manuelpillai offers it all, and asks tough questions in the process. None more so than in 'after being called a paki', which begins in quiet innocuity under the shadow of its title: 'my father used to say / the hardest oranges to peel / are often the sweetest'. This is a terrifyingly important poem whose minute stanzas and complete lack of punctuation lay the foundations for a heart-breaking final arrest:

tonight when I tell
my father what happened
he covers his mouth
with his hand
an orange peel attaching
back onto an orange

The poems in *Mutton Rolls* will keep you on your toes, never quite settled. At one moment 'an orgasm is caught in the breeze' the next a man is pickpocketing a corpse after a tsunami 'quietly as though hiding it from the sky'. Magical.

Manuelpillai's voice is subtle and concerned with the edge of things, the fine lines between this and that, the gesture we might have missed, 'the lady to the right / casual as breathing... [who]... pulled her handbag close'. These are hairline fractures which will (believe me) explode into chasms as you return to the poems time and time again, as the poet – ever so slowly – insinuates a wider picture 'like a hurricane that hasn't hit yet'.

'Crufts', one of my favourite poems in the pamphlet, renders a kind of duel universe, one of a family living room (in which an older relative is dying) and one of the dog show Crufts on the television. The process of grief, or maybe more pertinently, of coming to terms with death, 'they're arguing about what he should or shouldn't / eat', is enmeshed with the banality of the show, 'Mike is a three-year-old Irish Water Spaniel', until you're not quite sure where one ends and the other begins: 'they pull the leash so / tight it's choking the poor thing'. This is a special kind of world-building. But it is the way the poem leaves its world, its room, escaping for a second,

which got me: 'I shouldn't be doing this at the kitchen sink   crying / I mean'. And then a truly startling image assembles: 'neither should my cousin... nor / my mother who appears behind us   motionless   a family / photo   developing in the window'.

Mutton Rolls makes for an exhilarating read: an important new voice.

John Montague

John Montague: Selected Poems, 1961–2017, Ed. Peter Fallon
(Gallery Press) £12.50
Reviewed by Brian Morton

If Seamus hadn't become so famous, John Montague, who was a decade older, would be considered the premier Ulster poet of the last sixty years. There are close parallels between the two but Montague's republicanism and strong attraction to American and European models – he studied at Yale and the Iowa Writers' Workshop and died in Nice in 2016, a knight of the Légion d'honneur – tended to complicate his reputation.

America was a kind of return. Montague's father had gone there from County Tyrone in 1925, followed three years later by his mother and two older brothers. John was born in Brooklyn, but sent home to Ireland at four, in 1933. In 'The Locket' he confesses a sense of profound betrayal and rejection, softened only by the discovery, after her death, that Molly had worn his infant portrait next to her heart for most of her life. A yet more profound division afflicted young John, separating him from the language he had begun, as he says in 'A Flowering Absence' 'to dolphin delight in'. Mocked by a teacher for his Brooklyn slum vowels, he develops a stammer: 'my tongue became a rusted hinge / until the sweet oils of poetry // eased it and grace flooded in.'

A good deal of the poetry, and a high proportion of the poems selected here by Montague's long-time editor, Peter Fallon, are concerned with the aegis and nature of poetry itself. There are other poems, notably 'A Grafted Tongue', devoted to the sense of severance and shame young John felt at not being able to speak like his peers, but others again make use of impediment – distinctive line-lengths and stanza-breaks – to actualise the emergence of a poetic voice. In 'A Bright Day', addressed to John McGahern, he talks of 'a slow exactness // Which recreates experience / By ritualizing its details –'. In 'Hearth Song', this time dedicated to Heaney, he likens the emergence of poetry to the song of a cricket in the flags beneath his feet, 'Composed for no one, a tune / dreamt up under a flat stone, / earth's fragile, atonal rhythm', with a boy's glimpse of the alien creature, a 'minute, manic cellist' down in the stones. And there's a further shared parallel in 'The Country Fiddler' with Heaney's signature 'Digging' that poetry is a displaced inheritance; Heaney's father digs potatoes while upstairs and in apparent comfort his son delves in language; a fiddle left by a Montague uncle, once celebrated for song, rots away in the rafters until the boy again finds relief in verse.

Returning to Ireland propelled John back into an earlier state of being, almost primeval compared to Brooklyn's trolley lines and electricity. This wasn't just a generic juxtaposition of urban and rural, but something written to a far longer scale. The characters that people the poems are distant and monumental. 'Like dolmens round my childhood', solitaries who live with animal familiars or hereditary blindness or the foolishness of Billy Eagleson, who married a Catholic servant girl 'When all his Loyal family passed on' and suffered the noisy ostracism reserved for those who cross such lines. 'The Hill of Silence' from *Mount Eagle* is a shared ascent of stony terrain, the 'slope of loneli-

ness' where wounded myth-warriors might have their wounds tended. Ireland is full of such places.

Shamed for his vowels as a boy, Montague has been praised for them ever since. His poetry has a distinctive music, built round open-mid and close-mid back vowels, Irish diphthongs and stresses. Less often remarked, though, is the rhythmic accenting of consonants and a steady use of alliteration, which tends to highlight the atavistic monumentality of his landscapes and their population. In 'Like Dolmens Round My Childhood', he follows 'Fomorian fierceness of family and local feud' with 'Gaunt figures of fear and friendliness' which sounds like it might be reaching for Old English epic effect.

The closer to home the characters, the more modestly scaled. James Montague's return to Ireland is a long dying fall. Molly's death is the end of a stoic self-denial. There is poignancy in father and son breaking journey in a pub in order to hear John's broadcast voice win eventual acknowledgement – 'Not bad' – from the father, 'at ease, at last'. More striking still are the erotic poems and the taxonomising of a failed relationship that gather most prominently in *The Great Cloak*, where he draws on a *trouvere* spirit in 'Tearing' to actualise the pains of a modern relationship, its physicality unshirked. Heaney never managed anything of the kind and stumbled when he attempted it. There are few poems that more brilliantly capture the intensities of reunion than the transcontinental journey and meeting captured in 'All Legendary Obstacles' from the earlier *A Chosen Light:*

You had been travelling for days
With an old lady who marked
A neat circle in the glass
With her glove to watch us
Move into the wet darkness
Kissing, still unable to speak.

That might be said to be the key Montague moment, the half-beat before articulacy returns. It happens often in the verse, even when not explicitly referenced. The impediment wasn't just a reaction to shame. It was a cultural one, too.

Peter Fallon, who knows this work better than anyone, has done a wonderful job in sifting out the essence of Montague's. There's a lot from *A Chosen Field*, published in 1967 when he was newly confident in his voice, surprisingly less from 1972's *The Rough Field,* which remains the most personally revealing collection in terms of Montague's relations with his native/ not-native country, and a goodly amount from the collections that followed 1995's *Collected*, including the posthumous *Second Childhood,* which saw him going back to the riddle of having a mother and father but being motherless and fatherless, standing in a field alone and unable to express. Inevitably, these are all excerpts from a larger music. Montague's collections were not just accumulations of work, but careful orchestrations, sometimes symphonic, sometimes almost operatic. But the essence of him is here and will win him new readers.

Anywhere out of the world

Bell I Wake To, Patty Crane
(Zone 3 press) $14
Reviewed by David C. Ward

Regardless of what we do to it – from Instagram tourists to Australian brush fires – we persist in holding nature in our minds as an inviolate space, as something pure and untouched. Innocent, in a word. And instead of human-kind affecting (or destroying) nature, nature is still conceived as influencing, even healing us. The state of nature doesn't exist before society but alongside it as a counterpoint and a retreat from it. Poetically, this idealization has a long history not least because of man's history of near constant despoliation of pristine countryside. The Georgic and the pastoral were the felt response to a world that was too much with us and which was alienating us from ourselves. Nature, not Frost's family home, is where we go when we want to be taken in, connect and be made whole. As Patty Crane writes: 'If this land is the sermon, our hands in it/must be some kind of appeal.'

Crane lives in rural, western New England – aka Frost Country – and writes austere, measured poems about encounters with nature. Her range of vision is very close, honing-in on the small details to then zoom out to make a larger point. The opening of 'White Birch', 'I'd forgotten how the curled bark blushes pink sometimes,/out of dampness I suppose' leads to her daughter's nose bleed 'her hands cupped like leaves' to catch the blood and then finally connects to blood and a young girl maturing:'the blood / that's yet to come, her other flowering, wondering if she'll need me then.' The last line, 'It is the color of her needing me', is more hopeful and wistful than the reality often becomes, as the poet knows.

There's only slight suggestion of work and society in Crane's poems. 'Home Brigade' is a nice one about a neighbour who inadvertently sets the leaves on fire and calls for help: 'Little fires everywhere. / *I need help*, he said, / stomping out whatever flames he could. / I started stomping, too.' There's a lesson in self-reliance in 'how hard we worked / to keep from phoning for help. / A matter of foolish pride, or was it right? / The way we pulled together / …'. Other people – the neighbour, husband, children – are only lightly sketched in, disembodied against the natural world. The political or social world is similarly abstracted. The recipient of 'From a Letter to Yet Another Dead Civilian' is unspecified. The poem begins 'I have no answers / can barely speak' and then cuts to a description of a suddenly iced over pond, the movement of the water underneath the ice, and the salamanders who are released when holes are poked through it. Like the cloudy ice, the meaning is opaque, suggesting either blockage or evasion. A more directly horrifying

poem, 'And the Year Will be Late', describes a girl being stoned to death, site and time unspecified, and turned to stone after she is buried again. It ends with a swerve back to Massachusetts:

And under the apple trees
The fallen fruit is bronzed
But soft and softly sinking in.

It's not clear what this conclusion is supposed to achieve aside from ending the poem with a sigh. Since apples look a bit like stones and stones are part of nature too an opportunity seems to have been missed to indicate that the natural world is not Edenic.

In a series of poems about death and memory, Crane links nature and family in a way that is more complex, and satisfying, than her strictly descriptive poems. In 'Hospice':

Her arms   the branches
Her hands   the spring birds
carrying strands of her
off in their singing like that

The moment that a friend dies, her spirit leaving the hospice's room, 'Like those feathers we found arranged under a spruce, / as if the bird just lifted out of itself'. That transcendence is a nice touch and with her evident talent Crane should do more with it. Instead, she returns to home comforts: 'our snowy boots by the door, potato soup / steaming in the glazed blue bowls, / chairs dragged close to the fire.'

Baldwin's Catholic Geese

Baldwin's Catholic Geese,
Keith Hutson (Bloodaxe Books) £12
Reviewed by Rory Waterman

Keith Hutson is a writer for comedians, which explains the enticingly

odd focus of *Baldwin's Catholic Geese*. Most of the poems in this unusually fat debut collection are miniature life studies of and elegies for past stars of show business, usually of a less glamorous variety. Here, you'll learn about Georgie Doonan (1897–1973), who would kick his own arse to a drum beat ('Some critics called it / nothing but self-injury with rhythm'), the dad-o-gram ('Tell him three traits, and he'd impersonate / your dad'), and Alejandra Dominguez (1791–1833), '*Boneless in the Buff*', whose act would involve 'total collapse':

to form a pile of Puerto Rican flesh, // artiste-as-body-spill, barely above / the footlights, and her dark eyes, crablike, snug / inside the lowest naked fold, would look // this way, then that, at hundreds wondering where / her treasures were concealed […].

In some of these poems, the light touch belies something avaricious, animalistic, or just plain naff in the paying public; others are quick-cut with grim off-stage realities – such as when we learn about the nineteenth-century 'omnivore' who ate 'a chest of drawers each night' for audiences, between scene changes: 'In later life he fell apart – like / flatpacks do today – and died in a secure / unit chewing both his arms red raw.'

This poem exemplifies the intrigue of this book, but also some of its central failings: the enjambments are sloppy, the last phrase cliched, and the poem nothing more than its admittedly memorable anecdote. The best and tightest pieces here offer a fine raconteur's insights into the hustlers' world of kept-up appearances, in a way that speaks to and about those of us who earn our pay in the grey world of offices. But it can wear a bit thin, and it is hard not to feel that this is a superb pamphlet bloated into a chunky collection. 'You've got to leave 'em wanting more!', he writes, at the end of the final poem – but the book is likely to leave you wanting fewer poems that do more, which isn't the same thing. Too many of its too many poems fizzle out inconsequentially, or repeat one another in essence if not in language. Some flail for little pat, plain epiphanies that don't do much to make us think for ourselves: in the poem about the arse-kicker, it is that 'I'd have laughed, which won't surprise / you if you've ever run on joy alone'; in a poem about the once phenomenally popular singer Lottie Collins (1865–1910) it is 'how can we, / from here, salute you now? There's just one way, / with all we've got: *Ta-ra-ra- Boom-de-day!*'

This is anything but a glib book, though: it is a paean to making the best of what you've got, and to making hay while the sun shines, and its saving grace is its warmth and inherent originality. It cuts across the traditional grain of two hundred or so years of British history. Every poem comes with a sprightly note about its subject, and perhaps the greatest lasting pleasure this book will give you is several hours disappearing down internet rabbit holes as you shadow the author's impressive research.

Poetry Into Poetry

Last Dream, Giovanni Pascoli.
Ed. and trans. by Geoffrey Brock
(World Poetry Books) $16
Reviewed by Edmund Prestwich

Giovanni Pascoli is said to be much loved in Italy, though I'd hardly read him before this book. Tibor Wlassics describes him as 'the first Italian poet to "wring the neck" of elo-

quence' – in other words of inflated nineteenth century rhetoric. Different as they are, Pascoli and Gabriele D'Annunzio are sometimes described as the twin founders of modern Italian poetry. Pascoli's emotional tone is muted, his range limited, his style generally that of an exquisite miniaturist, but Geoffrey Brock's selection and translations have made me feel the power and beauty of his work, and that he's well worth further exploration.

These poems are essentially lyrical and contemplative. At the heart of most is a scene, a rural landscape, a garden, a seascape, whose life and movement are held within the stillness of the poet's wondering gaze and imbued with a sense of restrained but intense emotion. Sometimes there are elements of narrative. These may be no more than cryptic allusions to the tragic circumstances of the poet's early life, about which Brock's short concluding essay 'My Pascoli' tells us a little, or they may involve more explicit reminiscences, as in 'The Kite', where reminiscences of kite-flying at boarding school are interwoven with descriptions of landscape and the memory a schoolfellow who died as a child. Or in 'The Sleep of Odysseus' the whole narrative of the *Odyssey* becomes the unspoken background to a series of vignettes describing what Odysseus might have seen as his ship neared Ithaca after his visit to Aeolus's floating island if only he'd woken before his men opened the bag of the winds. Always, though, the core of the poem is wondering contemplation and the suggestion of emotion, usually by indirect means.

The delicacy of Pascoli's art lays peculiar burdens on the translator. Perhaps that's why he's not better known in Britain. In this way, Brock's gifts are just what we needed. He works by poetic recreation rather than step by step

translation. Sometimes he makes free with details. He seems to believe, as I do, that there's not much point in verse translations that don't convince as poems in their own right. Verse form and the suggestiveness of sound are crucial to a poetry that works as much by suggestion and implication as Pascoli's does. Where the translator falls short in this regard, the poem loses essential life. Of course Brock isn't uniformly successful. Although 'The Kite' is still poignant in his version, I feel that the intense demands of the terza rima rhyme scheme have led to a loss of strength through hints of padding and weak phrasing. But with most of these poems there's no sense of reading at second hand, trying to deduce an original from a diminished reproduction. Reading this from the beginning of 'My Evening':

The day was full of lightning,
but now the stars will come,
the quiet stars

or this from 'Night-Blooming Jasmine':

All through the night the flowers flare,
scent flowing and catching the wind,

I felt I was reading lines that danced flawlessly on their own feet, testifying both to the power of Pascoli's creation and to the fineness of Brock's own auditory expressiveness.

Readers with fair Italian can enjoy the facing originals alongside the translations and independently of them. They're not always easy though – Pascoli's descriptive precision comes partly from his use of precise nomenclature and often involves using dialect or otherwise rare words. I'd have found linguistic notes and a glossary useful in this regard.

Contributors

Robert Minhinnick co-founded the environmental charity, 'Sustainable Wales/Cymru Gynaliadwy' which he helps administer. His latest book from Carcanet is *Diary of the Last Man* (2017). **Maureen N. McLane**'s most recent book is *What I'm Looking For: Selected Poems* (Penguin, 2019). She lives for now in semi-lockdown in New York State. **Matthias Fechner** (b. 1966) undertook undergraduate and graduate studies at Stuttgart and Manchester Universities and completed his PhD at Sheffield University; he is currently associate researcher (DFG/FoIni RP) on contemporary poetry at Trier University, Germany. **Jena Schmitt** lives in Sault Ste. Marie, Ontario, Canada, with her children. Her poetry, short fiction and essays have appeared in journals in Canada and the UK. **Richard Gwyn**'s translation of Darío Jaramillo's poetry, *Impossible Loves*, is published by Carcanet. 'With Lowry in Cuernavaca' is from his forthcoming memoir, *Ambassador of Nowhere: A Latin American Pilgrimage*. **Oliver Dixon** is the author of *Human Form*. His most recent publications are reviews in *The High Window* and *Poetry Review* and a poem in *Tears in the Fence*. **Sharron Hass** lives in Tel Aviv and has published five collections of poetry. *The Day After* was published as a small-format book in 2018. She teaches in the Creative Writing Program at Tel Aviv University. **Gabriel Levin**'s most recent collection of poems *Errant* appeared with Carcanet in 2018. He lives in Jerusalem. **Nyla Matuk** is the author of *Stranger* and *Sumptuary Laws*, and a contributor to *New Poetries VI*. Her work appears in Canada, the UK., and the US. Canadian poet **Evan Jones** lives in Manchester. His latest collection is *Later Emperors* (Carcanet 2020). **Ian Pople**'s pamphlet *Spillway* is published by Anstruther Press, Toronto. A Cholmondeley Award winner, **John Greening**'s most recent collection is *The Silence* (Carcanet). He has edited Grigson, Blunden, Crichton Smith and several anthologies. His collected reviews, *Vapour Trails*, appear this autumn. **David C. Ward**'s *Call Waiting* was published by Carcanet in 2014. **Paul Stephenson**'s latest pamphlet is *Selfie with Waterlilies* (Paper Swans Press, 2017). He co-curates Poetry in Aldeburgh. **Katriona Feinstein** is an editor from London and has had her poems published in *Agenda*. She found the courage to start writing after the death of her poet grandmother in September 2019.

Colophon

Editors
Michael Schmidt
John McAuliffe

Editorial Manager
Andrew Latimer

Editorial Assistant
Charlotte Rowland

Contributing Editors
Vahni Capildeo
Sasha Dugdale
Will Harris

Design
Cover and Layout
by Emily Benton Book Design

Editorial address
The Editors at the address on the right. Manuscripts cannot be returned unless accompanied by a stamped addressed envelope or international reply coupon.

Trade distributors
NBN International

Represented by
Compass IPS Ltd

Subscriptions—6 issues
INDIVIDUAL–print and digital: £39.50; abroad £49
INSTITUTIONS–print only: £76; abroad £90
INSTITUTIONS–digital only: from Exact Editions (https://shop.exacteditions.com/gb/pn-review) to: PN Review, Alliance House, 30 Cross Street, Manchester, M2 7AQ, UK.

Supported by

Supported using public funding by
ARTS COUNCIL ENGLAND